marques vickers
2019-20

TWISTED TOUR GUIDE
SAN FRANCISCO BAY AREA
SHOCKING DEATHS, SCANDAL AND VICE

TWISTED TOUR GUIDE TO THE SAN FRANCISCO BAY AREA

SHOCKING DEATHS, SCANDALS AND VICE

By Marques Vickers

**MARQUIS PUBLISHING
HERRON ISLAND, WASHINGTON**

Version 1.1

Published by Marquis Publishing
Herron Island, Washington
TwistedTourGuides.com

Vickers, Marques, 1957

TWISTED TOUR GUIDE TO THE SAN FRANCISCO
BAY AREA
Shocking Deaths, Scandals and Vice

Dedication: To my daughters Charline and Caroline.

TABLE OF CONTENTS

Preface

EAST BAY AREA

Lovelle Mixon: A Desperate Final and Fatal Gamble Towards Escape

Oaks Card Club: Historic Gaming Surviving Amidst an Expansive Environment

The Oikos University Massacre: Piecing Together a Disjointed Puzzle

Oscar Grant III: When The Facts Behind a Killing Become Secondary

The Patty Hearst Kidnapping: The Final Nail into the Coffin of Idealism

Pleasanton Hotel: Alternating Naming Rights in a Desperate Town

Jockey Ron Hansen: Speed Killed

Ted Kaczynski: To Arms Against A Faceless Society and Enemy

The USS Hornet: Death On Board

Wagon Wheel Gambling Hall: The Cesspool That Was El Cerrito

MARIN COUNTY

Artie and Jim Mitchell: Contemporary Cain and Abel

Blue Rock Inn: From Resort to Scandal to Cornerstone

Litchfield's: A Solitary Neon Sign Conveying a Forgotten Legacy

The Marin County Courthouse Shootout: Thirty Minutes That Forever Altered Courtroom Security Procedures

David Carpenter: The Devil Behind Bifocals and a Stutter

The Marin County Barbeque Murders

Robin Williams: The Self-Destructive Tears of a Harlequin

Sally Stanford's Gilded Age

My appreciation to the following media outlets providing critical research details:

Online archives of the San Francisco Chronicle, San Francisco Examiner, San Francisco Call, Los Angeles Times, San Mateo Tribune, San Jose Mercury News, Oakland Tribune, Marin Independent Journal, Press Democrat, East Bay Times, New York Times, Washington Post, Napa Register, The Californian, The Guardian, Fresno Bee, Times Standard, SFWeekly, DailyMail.co.uk, Benicia Herald, New York Daily News newspapers, TheEpiphanyCenter.org, ChauceyBaileyProject.org, Wikipedia.org, MindControlBlackassassins.com, FBI.gov, KQED.org, CrimeLibrary.com, Hoodline.com, KlaasKids.org, SanJose.com, AliveEastBay.com, OAC.Cdlib.org, Murderpedia.com, Independent.com, KTVU.org, YouTube.com, DiscoverTheNetworks.org, YesMagazine.org, About.com, Fdsauk.freeforums.org, California Department of Corrections and Rehabilitation Inmatelocator.cdcr.ca.gov, WoodTV.com, Pinterest.com, MostWantedHoes.com, CityRating.com, CountryHomesOfAmerica.com, Websleuths.com, CodysInvestigations.com, Edhat.com, AJC.com, CNN.com, CBSNews.com, The Huffington Post, SourceOfTitle.com, Pineconearchive.com, Cielodrive.com, Biography.com, Berkeley.edu, The Atlantic Magazine, Britannica.com, TheZebraProject.blogspot.com, *Zebra* by Clark Howard, EvilBeings.com, Murderfacts.com, FoundSF.com, Sonomamag.com, HistorySMC.org, HauntedBay.com, ABC News7, Rockandrollroadmap.com, SonomaCounty.com, SantaRosaHistory.com, Cameronspub.net, DavidRumsey.com, Cameronhouse.org, Patch.com, TheFatLadyRestaurant.com, AtlasObscura.com, BeniciaLibrary.org, NancyPratt.com, HistorySMC.org, TheEpiphanycenter.org,

Photography shot between 2015-2019. Some of the locations may have altered with time and ownership changes. Many of the locations are still privately inhabited. Please don't disturb the residents.

Preface:

Avoid The Tourist Herds.

What could be more uninspiring than seeing the identical attractions that everyone else has for decades?

This Twisted Tour Guide escorts you to the places locals don't want to talk about anymore...the same places people once couldn't stop talking about. Long after the screaming headlines and sensationalism has subsided, these bizarre, infamous and obscure historical sites remain hidden awaiting rediscovery.

Each visitation site in this guide is accompanied by a story. Many of the narratives defy believability, yet they are true. The profiled cast of characters feature saints and sinners (with emphasis towards the latter).

Notorious crimes, murders, accidental deaths, suicides, kidnappings, vice and scandal are captivating human interest tales. Paranormal activity in the aftermath is common.

The photography from each profile showcases the precise location where each event occurred. The scenes can seem ordinary, weird and sometimes very revealing towards clarifying the background behind events.

If you're seeking an alternative to conventional tourism, this Twisted Tourist Guide is ideal. Each directory accommodates the restless traveler and even resident looking for something unique and different. You will never imagine or scrutinize the San Francisco Bay area through rose tinted glasses again.

The 101 California Building Rampage: Victims of Chance by a Deadly Rampage

At 2:57 p.m. on July 1, 1993, 55-year-old southern California mortgage broker and unsuccessful real estate speculator Gian Luigi Ferri entered the high-rise office building at 101 California Street in San Francisco. Dressed in a dark business, carrying an attaché case and wheeling a lawyer's case on a dolly, he resembled one of the building's practicing professionals and associates. Ferri resolutely entered an elevator to the 34th floor and the offices of the law firm of Pettit and Martin.

Exiting the elevator on the 34th floor, his intentions were precise and oriented towards combat. Ferri donned a pair of ear protectors and removed his sports coat. His battle armaments included multiple semi-automatic pistols and hundreds of rounds of ammunition including dozens of magazines carried in his lawyer cases. It was certain he had no personal exit strategy except death.

Without uttering a word, he entered the law offices and indiscriminately began firing at anyone and everyone in his sighting. He exited the office and after roaming the 34th floor, he then moved down one floor through an internal staircase and continued shooting. The carnage continued as he descended several floors.

Eight people were killed and six others injured during his shooting spree. Over 110 San Francisco police offices responded and shut off the alarms, which ultimately trapped Ferri between the 29th and 28th floor. He viewed his own demise with officers mounting the stairs and fired one shot into his chin killing himself instantly.

Ferri had been a client of Pettit and Martin over a dozen years prior to the shootings. He nursed an irrational grudge against the firm over their advice provided on certain real estate purchases regarding several trailer parks in Indiana and Kentucky. He had apparently no further contact with the firm since then. His life had steadily unraveled and he was deeply in debt. Two of his victims were lawyers with the firm Ferri blamed for his financial downfall. Neither had anything remotely to do with that advice.

His other victims were all unknown to the killer. None of the dead or wounded was on a personal hit list he carried in his attaché of more than 30 names. The list was composed reportedly of criminals, rapists, racketeers and lobbyists. A rambling letter found on Ferri's body bemoaned his perception of being victim to a system out to crush him. Aside from his blame towards Pettit and Martin, the four-page typed letter included rants about monosodium glutamate, the Food and Drug Administration, and the legal profession.

The dead included Deborah Fogel, a secretary for the law firm Davis, Wright and Tremaine, four employees of Pettit and Martin: John C. Scully, an associate lawyer in the firm, Allen J. Berk, a law partner, David Sutcliffe, a summer legal assistant, a secretary, Shirley Mooser and Donald Michael Merrill, whose reason for being in the building were unclear. Jack Berman was a partner with the firm Bronson, Bronson and McKinnon who was art the offices to attend a deposition of his client Jody Sposato also killed. Injured in the attack were Vicky Smith, Sharon Jones O'Roke, Brian F. Berger, Deanna Eaves and Charles Ross. John Scully was mortally wounded while heroically thrusting himself in the line of fire in front of his wife Michelle, who was also shot in the arm.

The shootings renewed calls nationwide for tighter gun control. The publicity from the senseless killings was followed by a number of legal and legislative actions. In the immediate aftermath, a California judge repealed a law that had given gun manufacturers immunity against lawsuits from shooting victims and their relatives. The victims of the massacre filed a collective lawsuit again the Florida based gun manufacturer of Ferri's weaponry.

Eight hushed years later, with the bloodstains long washed away and the bullet holes repaired, the California Supreme Court ruled against gunshot victims (and their survivors). Further, future victims were prohibited from suing gun manufacturers for injuries done to them by someone using one of their weapons. Another team of faceless and victimless lawyers had ultimately prevailed in these proceedings. The debate continues amongst a divided nation, still unresolved. Gun abuse continues to reign legally within the United States.

The Pettit and Martin law firm has long ceased operations at 101 California, unable to recover from the notoriety. Another law firm leases and operates from their suite. Visitors to the 101 California office building circulate freely throughout the lobby with security in evidence. Daily many enter elevators without scrutiny. Business and risk have returned to normal.

101 California Building
101 California Street, 34th Floor, San Francisco

Sublime: Overindulgence Slays The Golden Goose

In mid 1996, the music group Sublime was on the cusp of international recognition and stardom. Their third album *Killin' It* had just been released and the music industry was taking notice. Lead singer Bradley James Nowell typified the band's raucous and rowdy behavior. His charisma and powerful vocals had elevated the band into one of the most popular live acts in Southern California. Their music was classified as *ska*. Band members simply considered themselves *punkers*.

Nowell, born and raised in Long Beach, had played in various local groups before forming Sublime with bassist Eric Wilson and drummer Bud Gaugh. They had met while attending Cal State Long Beach. Throughout the band's rise and tenure, Nowell struggled with heroin abuse. He superficially appeared to be handling the group's acclaim well, particularly following the birth of his son. He married the mother Troy Dendekker on May 18, 1996.

One week later, the band set out on a five-day tour of Northern California. A European and East Coast tour was scheduled to follow. At the Phoenix Theatre in Petaluma, the band played what would become their final concert.

Returning to their accommodations, then called the Ocean View Motel adjacent to the San Francisco coastline, the trio crashed from exhaustion and overindulgence. Nowell had unsuccessfully attempted to awaken each band members to go with him for a walk on the beach. Gaugh awoke in the late morning to discover Nowell lying prostrate on the floor next to his bed with his pet Dalmatian *Lou Dog* whimpering.

Nowell remained unresponsive with a yellow film around his mouth. It became apparent he had overdosed on heroin and had died several hours earlier.

Two months later, their album was renamed *Sublime* and four of the tracks became staples on radio playlists. Their videos displaying concert footage received mainstay rotation on MTV. Their raw performance passion elevated their status into the band *everyone wanted to see* during 1997. The album sold over six million copies. Absent of their charismatic lead singer, their momentum braked to a halt. The group was relegated to releasing previously recorded material on future compilation albums. The party was over.

According to Nowell in magazine interviews *we were taking heroin to be more creative*. There was nothing particularly novel in his ultimate demise except the inopportune timing. Numerous self-destructive performers have emulated his accidental death. What the group Sublime might have attained remains adrift to speculation. An attempt to reform and tour with another lead singer in 2009 stalled.

The Ocean View Motel has since been renamed the Sea Scape Inn. Its notoriety has diminished along with Bradley James Nowell's cautionary tale of excess.

Ocean View Motel (Renamed Sea Scape Inn), 45340 Judah Street, San Francisco

The 1937 Atherton's Brothel Report: Naming Names

In a March 1937 article published by William Randolph Hearst's *San Francisco Examiner*, it was reported that the city had hired private investigator Edwin Atherton to investigate police graft. Atherton's findings provided a grand jury with a list of 135 addresses actively engaged in prostitution. The territory included the South of Market, Western Addition and North Beach.

Many of the itemized structures remain today employed in different capacities. The Western Addition based buildings have been razed and replaced by affordable income housing developments.

The *Atherton Report* uncovered massive police misconduct including gambling, prostitution, bribed elections, illicit bail bond practices, and significant payoffs filtered through the San Francisco Police department.

The two most affected individuals outside of law enforcement were Madam Dolly Fine and bail bondsman Peter McDonough. Once the report was released, Fine's phones were wiretapped and her properties raided. She ultimately lost the bulk of her fortune before mysteriously disappearing before a mandated court appearance. She was reportedly sighted by Chicago police in 1938, but vanished the same day.

Peter McDonough and his brother had become multi-millionaires through their bail bond enterprise, the first such practice nationally beginning in 1898. McDonough was considered by police to be a major local crime boss. The extent of their operations was labeled by Atherton as *The Fountainhead of Corruption*.

Early in his career, McDonough had skirted legal inquiries but was finally incarcerated for bootlegging during Prohibition in Alameda County for eight months. He was imprisoned briefly in 1938 for refusing to discuss his role in police corruption and forfeited his bail bond license. In 1941, he appealed the decision via the California Insurance Commissioner. In October 1942, the Commissioner denied his appeal without a hearing. The following year, the California Supreme Court likewise denied his petition. He died in 1947 having never successfully regained his status.

Edwin Atherton's professional trajectory began in the consular service where during World War I he served in Italy, Bulgaria and Jerusalem. After the war, he was assigned to Canada before resigning to take a position with the Department of Justice. He headed the San Francisco bureau from 1925 to 1927. His service with the Bureau of Investigation (later renamed the FBI) resulted in the 1924 capture of a neo-revolutionary army of Mexican nationals under the command of General Enrique Estrada along the Mexican-California border.

He resigned in 1927 to form a Los Angeles based private investigation firm with another special agent, Joseph Dunn. Ten years later, their firm was hired by the City of San Francisco. His findings generated national headlines.

In 1938, he was hired to thoroughly investigate the Pacific Coast Conference. Two years later, he was appointed as the PCC's High Commissioner to carry out his recommended reforms. In July 1944, he was hospitalized at Santa Monica Hospital for a month before eventually dying at 47 from a gall bladder illness.

Atherton Reads List Of Resorts to Jury

ROSTER SAID TO INCLUDE ALL LEADING PLACES

Edwin N. Atherton, graft investigator, last night read to the grand jury a list of known houses of prostitution operating in San Francisco. This list, he said, included all of the more notorious resorts which were in operation between five and nine months ago.

Here is the list submitted to the jury by Atherton:

808 Broadway	106 Fern	857 Kearny	1509 Pine
513 Broadway	944 Fillmore	917 Kearny	841 Polk
517 Broadway	1029 Fillmore	1006 Kearny	611½ Post
527 Broadway	1831 Fillmore	1032 Kearny	1045 Post
584 Broadway	184 Fourth	1032½ Kearny	1876 Post
616 Broadway	702 Franklin	1046 Kearny	666 Sacramento
672 Broadway	450 Geary	1054 Kearny	37 Sixth
691 Broadway	726 Geary	633 Larkin	41 Sixth
705 Broadway	924 Geary	923 Larkin	43 Sixth
716 Broadway	1036 Geary	926 Larkin	102 Sixth
730 Broadway	1514 Geary	237 Leavenworth	148 Sixth
1275 Bush	1516 Geary	379 Leavenworth	220 Sixth
1582 Bush	1573 Geary	1518 Market	221 Sixth
585 California	1761 Geary	977 McAllister	1303 Steiner
621 California	1769 Geary	52 McAllister	1133 Stockton
669 Clay	680 Golden Gate	253 Mason	1218 Stockton
42 Columbus	734 Golden Gate	379 Minna	1224 Stockton
67 Columbus	871 Golden Gate	857 Montgomery	1238 Stockton
248 Columbus	1019 Golden Gate	215 O'Farrell	1323 Stockton
331 Columbus	822 Hyde	337 O'Farrell	1411 Stockton
301½ Columbus	855 Hyde	587 O'Farrell	1230 Sutter
371 Columbus	531A Jackson	793 O'Farrell	1969 Sutter
444 Columbus	535 Jackson	426 Pacific	730 Taylor
575 Columbus	178 Jones	534 Pacific	51 Turk
44 Eddy	515 Jones	578 Pacific	74 Turk
74 Eddy	331 Jones	611 Pacific	116 Turk
168 Eddy	333 Kearny	619 Pacific	140 Turk
333 Eddy	466 Kearny	623 Pacific	1231 Turk
486 Eddy	523 Kearny	637 Pacific	725 Vallejo
1343 Eddy	551 Kearny	645 Pacific	1201 Webster
255 Ellis	638 Kearny	528 Pine	1232 Webster
1506 Ellis	808 Kearny	530 Pine	1563 Webster
1563 Ellis	821 Kearny	1563 Pine	632 Van Ness

March 1937 *San Francisco Examiner* issue

508 Broadway Street (Later Finocchio's Nightclub)

513-517 Broadway Street

527 Broadway Street

1275 Bush Street

1582 Bush Street

Chambers Mansion: Dispelling Mythology From Fancy

Haunted mansions are far from an anomaly in San Francisco's Pacific Heights district. The Chambers Mansion is fronted by an imposing iron gate and protective shrubbery making access and viewing challenging. The mint green and white trimmed Victorian blends seamlessly and nearly invisibly into the neighborhood's architecture.

The house was constructed in 1887 for Robert Craig Chambers who reportedly made his fortune in Utah silver mines. He had sold his Ontario silver mine near Park City to George Hearst, father of newspaper icon William Randolph. His wife Eudora lived with him along with later two of her nieces, Lillian and Harriet. Eudora preceded him in death in 1897 following a bizarre newspaper account of her mysterious weeklong disappearance and later attempted suicide along the Valencia Street railroad tracks.

Her cause of death nor her final resting place has ever been revealed.

Upon Robert Chamber's own demise from appendicitis in 1901, the property was passed on to his sister and remained within the family for decades. In the 1970s, under new ownership, it was converted into a 15-room luxury hotel property and hosted evening magic and private concert performances. In 2000, the Mansion Hotel was sold to a private developer and converted into two townhouses.

Fact and fanciful legend have taken divergent directions regarding the mansion's history and supposed haunting. The most often repeated is that Robert (not Richard as he is erroneously called) deeded the house to his nieces in his will. He has often been described as a U.S. Senator yet the only traceable evidence of elected office is that he was once a Plumas County sheriff between 1858-62. Adding confusion to the claim is that Utah did not become a state until nearly ten years after his arrival in San Francisco.

A fabricated story continues acknowledging that the two live-in nieces detested each other and one (always unnamed) built an adjoining house to reside in. The other, named Claudia remained in the mansion until she was tragically and gruesomely killed. The inventive account confirms that she was nearly sawed in half in a *farm implementation accident*.

This incredulous myth has been spread like manure as fact in customarily reliable reporting outlets. If the credibility and details seem strained...they merely are.

Chambers Mansion:
2220 Sacramento Street, San Francisco

The CIA's Sex and LSD Playhouse

Operation Midnight Climax was an ultra secret CIA program operating in San Francisco between 1955 until 1965. The funded program's objective was oriented towards developing substances that would oblige subjects to reveal their secrets. Staged on the north side of Telegraph Hill, an elegant modernist apartment with panoramic views became the agency's base of operation.

San Francisco prostitutes would lure unsuspecting clients from nearby North Beach bars to the Chestnut Street building and then dose the men with LSD using foods, drinks and cigarettes. The intent was to stimulate revealing conversations. The prostitute's services were paid partially with barter accounts they could cash in to evade future incarceration. CIA personnel would then view the subsequent sexual activities and accompanying conversations through a two-way mirror reportedly sipping martinis.

The program had its origins during World War II through the Office of Strategic Services (the agency's predecessor). A concentrated liquid form of marijuana was induced into a New York mobster who revealed far more than the program administrators anticipated. These results prompted further research.

At the height of the communist *red scare*, mind control experiments were being conducted globally. The Korean War accentuated reports of communist brainwashing and the film *The Manchurian Candidate* heightened the paranoia. It is speculated that experimental drugs were administered to forgotten individuals such as imprisoned POWs, mental patients, criminals, addicts and prostitutes.

Hundreds of scientists were clandestinely participating in the research.

The 1943 development of the powerful drug LSD opened a new chapter in espionage potential. A young chemist named Sidney Gottlieb persuaded CIA official Richard Helms (future director of the bureau) to authorize the drug as a spy tool. In 1953, CIA director Allen Dulles approved such a program for the *covert use of biological and chemical materials*.

The program wavered beyond control initially. Gottlieb, known as the *Black Sorcerer* and *Dirty Trickster* began administering LSD and other hallucinogenic drugs to unwitting subjects. In 1953, Gottlieb dosed CIA colleague Frank Olson, stimulating a mental crisis that ended in Olson falling to his death from a 10th-floor window. Protocol required a brief pause, but Gottlieb continued to supervise preparations of lethal poisons and mind control potions under the guise of national security.

Gottlieb retired from the CIA in 1972 confessing that his work had been *ineffective*. His retirement life may have been a period of questioning the morality of his past (debatable). He began advocating peace and environmentalism. He and his wife spent 18 months operating a leper hospital in India. He spent his final years caring for the dying at a hospice. He died quietly in March 1999 at his home in Washington, Virginia.

The San Francisco LSD Sex House became the West Coast branch of the program also operating in Greenwich Village. One of the more intriguing observations was the period of time when a man proved most emotionally vulnerable. The postcoital stage tended to stimulate the most revealing exchanges.

The program experimented with other controlled substances and ethical scrutiny appeared absent. The program might have continued longer, but when the CIA's inspector general stumbled upon the *safe house* program, he mandated their closure. The Chestnut Street program was terminated in 1965. There is no tally on how many lives and minds these unethical activities damaged.

The CIA's documentation regarding this program has never been publicly disclosed and the files are probably destroyed. *New York Times* revelations about the CIA's illegal spying on Americans were first published in 1974.

It would seem a relief that a government agency would ultimately regulate themselves from crossing ethical boundaries. In our current cynical age, secrecy issues involved with cell phone conversations and cyberspace raise fresh concerns as to whether privacy can even exist.

The intelligence gathering community has never exhibited a precedent for restraint. It may be naivety to imagine that confidentiality will ever legitimately exist.

**CIA's LSD and Sex Safe House:
225 Chestnut Street, San Francisco**

1885 Chinatown: Mapping Cultural Stereotypes

Ethnicity and racial profiling are sensitive subjects in contemporary society and rightly so. In the mid-1880s following the national financial *Panic of 1873*, many Americans viewed Chinese immigrants as employment threats to be feared. Two decades before, American government policies had encouraged Chinese immigration to help construct the transcontinental railroads. The work was laborious, conditions severe and poorly compensated. Despite the hardships and a subsequent series of discriminatory laws passed in the 1870s, Chinese communities congregated in urban centers that were typically labeled *Chinatowns*.

The paranoia reached its pinnacle with the passage of the Federal Chinese Exclusion Act of 1882 banning Chinese immigration. The new statute reduced the annual immigration quota from 40,000 in 1881 to 10 in 1887.

Amidst the fiery and inflammatory rhetoric, the San Francisco Supervisors authorized the creation of a detailed map of the Chinatown district in July 1885. Unlike any precedent documentation, this map included six differing colors to distinguish specific building uses. The most commonly employed color was light orange designating simple Chinese occupancy. Red indicated temples or buildings of worship.

Additional color designations became more detailed and biased intending to highlight the depravity of the culture. Orange represented gambling houses, yellow was for opium dens, green was for brothels with Chinese prostitutes and blue for brothels with *White* prostitutes.

Despite the overt racism, Chinatown residents were

governed principally by their own Tongs (secret societies) and not city hall based authorities. The Earthquake and Fire of 1906 changed everything. Few buildings remained standing following the catastrophe. Ruins were cleared and the neighborhoods required rebuilding and modified street realignments. Numerous members of the ruling Tongs, now destitute, returned to China. The formerly vice infected structures were converted into residential housing utilizing blueprints, building codes and masonry instead of inexpensive and hastily constructed clapboard. The district was modernized yet still retained distinctively cultural icons and ornamentation.

Slivers of modern Chinatown retain a mysterious edge. Tourists and outsiders rarely frequent these sunken alleyways that appear invisible in plain sight. Food and service businesses still operate behind the corridor front entrances. Not surprisingly, the majority of the pre-Earthquake vice trade thrived amidst this darkened environment.

It is inconceivable a similar 1885 Chinatown map could be published today accentuating a single nationality. It is equally improbable that the district will ever entirely resemble any other sector of San Francisco.

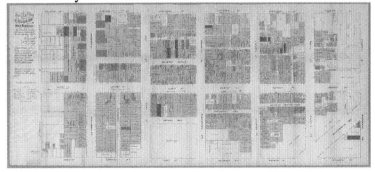

1885 Map of Chinatown Brothels and Gambling

Jason Court (formerly Sullivan's Alley)

Duncombe Alley

Beckett Alley (formerly Lozier Street)

The Cliff House and Sutro Baths: Ruin and Reincarnation

The Cliff House settles majestically on bluffs upon Point Lobos Avenue offering a panoramic view of the Pacific Ocean coastline, Seal Rocks and stark ruins of the once regal Sutro Baths. Five major incarnations have defined this extraordinarily but volatile location.

The initial construction in 1856 employed lumber that was salvaged from a ship trapped on the basalt cliffs below. The ships misfortune became the property owner's opportunity and a humble inauguration.

The second Cliff House was constructed in 1863 on a more spacious and upscale design catering to the San Francisco elite who enjoyed the privacy over champagne, and oysters. The journey from downtown was arduous and accomplished by a toll road or horseback, keeping the establishment isolated and the clientele affluent.

A decade later, Golden Gate Park opened. In 1877, the toll road, now Geary Street was purchased by the city and available for public access. Buslines, railways and streetcars accommodated larger crowds.

The upscale luster tarnished with this new mass intrusion. The Cliff House became noteworthy as a *French* restaurant, but not necessarily because of the cuisine. The property gradually transformed into a brothel getaway featuring *intimate* room service.

Adolph Sutro owned a small cottage nearby and abhorred the decadent neighborhood activities. An engineer and sound businessman, Sutro had amassed his fortune developing the mechanism for ventilating and draining

Comstock Lode mines. He purchased the Cliff House in 1883 and immediately transformed the property into a more staid and respectable resort.

On January 16, 1887, the schooner *Parallel* ran aground on the rocks below. The collision detonated the ship's cargo of explosive dynamite and black powder. Pieces of the ship were tossed in excess of a mile away. The entire north wing of the tavern was demolished by the blast, but later repaired. A defective flue ignited another inferno on Christmas night 1894 that destroyed the entire property.

In 1894 Sutro was elected Mayor of San Francisco and the following year began construction on a colossus seven-story Victorian Chateau upon the ashes. Locals referred to the structure as the *Gingerbread Palace*. He also began work on the Sutro Baths in a small cove immediately north of the property, which opened to the public on March 14, 1896.

The Sutro Baths included six gigantic indoor pools, a museum, a skating rink and numerous other recreational diversions. Sutro stocked both the Cliff House and Baths with an enormous collection of stuffed animals, artwork and historical artifacts. The complex was truly considered a *people's palace*. Sutro was extremely popular and a perpetual promoter. He was considered a *disappointing* mayor during his two-year term. Upon his death in 1898 at the age of 68, his extensive fortune and chaotic legal affairs prompted bitter disputes amongst his heirs.

The *Gingerbread House* survived the 1906 earthquake, but ultimately only lasted eleven years. On September 7, 1907, another crippling fire completely destroyed it.

Sutro's daughter, Dr. Emma Merritt commissioned a scaled down replacement restaurant on the site in a neo-classical style. It opened in 1909 and is the structure that remains today. The facility was promoted as a *great Bohemian restaurant*, but floundered, principally due to Prohibition. It was shuttered from 1925 to 1936 before being purchased by the owners of the nearby *Playland-at-the-Beach*. When that 10-acre amusement park struggled and closed in 1972, the National Park Service purchased the property. The restaurant is currently operated on a long-term lease serving food, drinks and scenic views of the headlands.

The Sutro Baths struggled financially for decades due to the exorbitant operating and maintenance costs. Eventually the baths were converted into an ice skating rink. In 1964, the property was sold to developers planning a high-rise apartment complex. The development never materialized. An arson fire destroyed the rink in the process of demolition. Curiously, the planned apartment developers left San Francisco with their blueprints and simply claimed the insurance money on the property.

What currently remains are accessible ruins from the site including concrete walls, blocked off stairs and passageways, and a tunnel with a profound crevice in the middle. The perspective from the Cliff House is as riveting as the eternally turbulent ocean waves.

It may be surmised that visionary Adolph Sutro's dreams collectively ended up in smoke. However, three of his gifts to San Francisco, Mount Sutro (originally Mount Parnassus), Sutro Tower and the Sutro Baths still celebrate his name and legacy.

Cliff House:
1090 Point Lobos Avenue, San Francisco

Sutro Baths:
1004 Point Lobos Avenue, San Francisco

A Strange Entanglement With A Killer Piano

The Condor nightclub has been a cultural icon on Broadway Street in North Beach since topless dancer and stripper Carol Doda gained international fame between the 1960s through early 80s. Aside from her international breast enlargement acclaim, one of her signature act entries was from a piano that descended fifteen feet from the club's ceiling.

A piano may seem a harmless enough prop, but for James *Jimmy the Beard* Ferrozzo, it proved lethal. On November 24, 1983 at approximately 4 a.m., longtime Condor employee Ferrozzo and his younger girlfriend boarded the piano with assumed carnal intimacy intentions. *Jimmy the Beard* presumably mounted her in the missionary position, but accidentally tripped the elevating lever to the piano.

For fifteen agonizing feet, the piano raised skyward. It is conceivable that Ferrozzo was too occupied to notice. The option of jumping off apparently never crossed his mind.

The levitating piano eventually squished Ferrozzo, reportedly fully clothed, onto the ceiling surface while he lay partially upon his beloved. It proved his final act of chivalry or stupidity. For over three hours, the couple remained sandwiched between the piano and ceiling. He expired and she continued to shriek and scream, but to no avail, unable to budge. A janitor arrived at 7:30 a.m. and finally freed them.

Jimmy the Beard doubtlessly never expected to make the front page of the *San Francisco Chronicle's* Thanksgiving Day edition. The story spread internationally for weeks afterwards due to its sheer improbability.

Today the Condor has returned to its striptease and erotic dancer roots following several years in the sportsbar wilderness. The killer piano along with *Jimmy the Beard's* girlfriend have vanished into oblivion. Following her official *dancing* retirement, Carol Doda opened an intimate lingerie shop called *Champagne and Lace* inside a niche location at 1850 Union Street. She operated the store until her death from kidney failure in 2015. The neon marquee adorning the Condor no longer showcases her profile, a melancholy omission for the woman who was a pioneer in another silicon based industry.

Condor Club:
560 Broadway Street, San Francisco

Curran Theatre: The Haunting Ticket Taker

On the evening of Tuesday November 28, 1933, theatergoers were waiting impatiently to take their seats for a revival of the hit musical *Show Boat* at the Curran Theatre. Only four performances remained for this initial San Francisco run and the house was sold out.

As described by witnesses, *a young, hollow-cheeked man with skittish eyes* shoved his way to the front of the box office line. Earlier in the day, 25-year old Eddie Anderson had held-up five different businesses locally amassing approximately $1,500.

Without demanding cash or uttering a word, Anderson pulled out a revolver and shot Hewlett Tarr who was manning the box office. Tarr, 25 years old was considered one of the Curran's most experienced employees having worked there for seven years following his graduation from Lowell High School. He was scheduled to meet his fiancé for dinner once the performance began. They had been engaged following a five-year relationship and their wedding was only weeks away.

The gunshot killed Tarr instantly. His fiancée had unexpectantly shown up to surprise him. She became so grief stricken upon hearing the news that she collapsed. Tarr's single mother who he supported with his income had to be briefly hospitalized.

Three weeks passed before San Francisco police apprehended Eddie Anderson. He claimed his robberies were motivated by his need to earn *easy income* to impress women and particularly his current girlfriend. His *girlfriend* denied that their relationship was romantic and they'd only known each other for three weeks. She adamantly denied that money could buy her love.

Anderson was put on immediate trial and pled *not guilty* citing that the trigger accidentally was activated upon being caught by the metal bars of the box office. Whether his excuse was plausible or even true, the jury reached a *guilty* verdict after deliberating only seven hours. Ten days after his capture, Tarr was sentenced to death by hanging at San Quentin.

Generations of Curran audiences have reported strange and eerie sounds throughout the theatre and apparitions of a strange figure in the lobby mirrors. The prime suspect has typically been Hewlett Tarr, even despite *Phantom of the Opera's* extended five-year run in the late 1990s.

Curran Theatre:
445 Geary Street San Francisco

Dan White: Political Killing and Suicide Solution

It is not an exaggeration to suggest that former San Francisco Supervisor Dan White may qualify as the city's most historically reviled political figure.

Nine days following the People's Temple massacre at Jonestown in Guyana, on November 27, 1978, White executed Mayor George Moscone and Supervisor Harvey Milk. The killings were calculated and cowardly with absolutely no remorse for the victims, their families or any subsequent consequences. In itself, the murders were reprehensible, but what followed at White's trial was considered one of the worst travesties of American justice.

White shot Moscone in his office because he had refused to re-appoint him to his seat on the Board of Supervisors. White had officially resigned over two weeks previously but changed his mind regarding the decision. Milk had lobbied heavily against his re-appointment and was a habitual adversary with White on city legislative issues.

San Francisco politics during the 1970s was turbulent and volatile with the nature of local representation undergoing a radical transformation. White and Milk were both elected during the 1977 election when district based representation was first introduced.

Before politics, White had been an acknowledged proudly as a local high school athletic star. He was a paratrooper during his Vietnam service and upon returning home, a San Francisco police officer and firefighter. He and his district aligned themselves with a slim majority that characterized the Board of Supervisor's pro-growth philosophy. White, however, often found himself isolated on issues that required a broader consensus and participation base. He was the lone contrary vote against the historic San Francisco gay rights ordinance passed in 1978.

White faced tremendous financial difficulties due to a failing restaurant he owned and his marginal salary as a supervisor. He was fed up with the workings of city politics and his exclusion from *insider* status. The accumulated stress from his circumstances, prompted him to resigned on November 10.

His resignation suited the designs of Moscone who leaned towards a more controlled, decentralized growth agenda. Moscone was empowered to appoint a successor and since White often constituted the swing vote on local issues, he would be able to exert his influential preferences towards the future direction of the city.

White's supporters urged him to rescind his resignation by requesting reappointment from Moscone and promised him some financial support. White appealed to the Mayor to re-appoint him. Moscone had little interest in such a decision and was lobbied heavily by more liberal city political interests.

Moscone ultimately decided to appoint Don Horanzy, a federal housing official. On the day he was planning to formally announce Horanzy as his replacement, White initiated his premeditated rampage.

Concealing his loaded police service revolver and ten rounds of ammunition in his coat pocket, White entered City Hall through a first floor window evading the building's metal detectors.

White began by entering Moscone's reception office and requested an appointment. It may be conceivable that he still thought his re-appointment prospects possible. Moscone immediately informed him of his decision clarifying any uncertainty. White began arguing heatedly with the Mayor who discreetly moved the conversation to his interior private lounge to avoid further public unpleasantness. Once inside, White removed his revolver and fired four rounds, including two into Moscone's temple killing him instantly.

White proceeded to his former office and intercepted Harvey Milk on the way. Milk agreed to join him in his office unaware of the preceding events. He was peppered with four shots before a conclusive fifth bullet was fired into his skull. Neither victim was armed nor had a premonition of White's motives.

Dan White left City Hall unchallenged and later that day turned himself in to a former police colleague. He maintained then and throughout his trial that the killings were not premeditated. The callousness of the acts confirmed otherwise.

White was tried for first-degree murder with special circumstances, which could have qualified him for the death penalty. At trial, his defense team miraculously recruited an intellectually challenged and gullible jury.

White's defense team claimed that he had been depressed, evidenced by, among other things, his eating of unhealthy junk foods. The defense argued that White's depression led to a state of mental diminished capacity, leaving him incapable of the necessary premeditation skills to commit first-degree murder. The jury accepted these arguments during their deliberations. White was found guilty of the lesser crime of voluntary manslaughter.

The verdict sparked outrage and riots in San Francisco, and eventually led to the California legislature abolishing the diminished capacity criminal defense.

White served a mere five years in prison for his double homicide before being paroled in 1984. He was obligated to live in the Los Angeles area during the tenure of his parole. He visited Ireland for several months once the parole expired. At 39, his reputation was forever blackened, his future prospects bleak and he was loathed by the hometown he loved.

His foundation had irreversibly crumbled. He considered himself a pariah and a burden to his immediate family. Living locally permanently was no longer a conceivable option. He felt sorry for the damage he had caused his family, yet still despite six years of reflection, couldn't bring himself to express remorse for the shootings.

Approximately eight and a half months after being released from prison, White inserted a rubber hose into his car parked in his small Excelsior district garage. With his car running, the hose piped lethal carbon monoxide inside. It was reported that behind the wheel he held photographs of his family as he silently slipped into unconsciousness. His suicide became the final desperate chapter of a doomed novel. His brother discovered the vehicle and body around mid-afternoon.

Few if any high profile individuals or politicians publicly mourned his demise. His death closed one the most tumultuous eras of San Francisco politics.

Today, the mere mention of Dan White still provokes disgust over the injustice of his sentence. Harvey Milk has become lionized as an iconic symbol of the gay rights movement. George Moscone is best known as the namesake for the city's convention center complex.

The San Francisco of today does not resemble Moscone's vision for the city. The post-Millennium vertical development of downtown San Francisco has trivialized the politically lethal discussions over growth policy from thirty-five years ago. History has shown that urban development ultimately prevails and eclipses any elected political body that attempts to control or moderate it.

San Francisco eulogized their murdered leaders symbolically. Ironically afterwards, the city followed the political agenda of their assassin.

San Francisco City Hall
1 Dr Carlton B Goodlett Place, San Francisco

Dan White's Residence:
150 Shantee Avenue, San Francisco

Diamond Jessie Hayman's Brothels

Nestled in today's perpetually declining Tenderloin district, *Diamond Jessie* Hayman's original three-story brothel during the late nineteenth century was the epitome of style, taste and sophistication. It featured fifteen lavishly furnished suites, three fireplaces and a renowned champagne cellar.

The tall, elegant and redheaded Jessie Mellon was born in New Orleans and began her own professional career as a prostitute working the Sierra Nevada mineral mines. Arriving in San Francisco in the late 1880s, she joined Nina Hayman *parlor* house and during their affiliation became the madam's favorite.

Near the end of 1898, her mentor Nina Hayman retired to marry a wealthy lumber dealer. She graciously ceded Jessie the business and as an honorarium, Jessie adopted surname. The practice flourished and Jessie expanded operations by purchasing additional tracts of real estate within San Francisco.

Each of her prostitutes was modeled in contemporary wardrobes featuring tailored suits, furs, and negligees. Her women received regular medical care. Her rates were reportedly the highest in the city. Her original location was destroyed in the 1906 San Francisco Earthquake and Fire. However her reputation was elevated in the aftermath when her employees reputedly passed out clothing and food to many left destitute by the tragedy.

Jessie Hayman could achieve nobility in flattery, but she preferred diamonds.

In the 1890s, Jessie was introduced by photographer Arnold

Genthe to a Grand Duke of the Imperial Russian Empire. The Grand Duke became immediately smitten and declared *she had the face and figure of an empress, and the pose and manner of one as well. Diamond Jessie* refused the Grand Duke's offer to accompany him back to Russia, but he insisted upon a noteworthy remembrance.

The Grand Duke commissioned a life-sized enlargement of her portrait, which he kept throughout his return voyage. The 1917 Bolshevik Revolution obscured the location of the portrait along with the Grand Duke's fate. The photographic negative was destroyed in the 1906 earthquake.

Hayman reportedly died in 1923 in an upscale London hotel at the age of 56, unmarried but lavishly jeweled in diamonds. Her will stipulated that her two pet cats Beppo and Teddy were entitled to one thousand dollars each. Beppo died a few days after Jessie and the surviving cat Teddy stopped eating. An addendum to the text designated that Belle Harte would inherit $1,000 to care for the cats. Although her photographic image has become obscure, her establishments (with a single exception) remain fixtures within the Tenderloin district.

Her destroyed brothel at 225 Ellis Street would become the future Coronado Saloon owned by the infamous Jerome Bassity.

Coronado Saloon
Jerome Bassity would establish his reputation as the *King of the Tenderloin* for nearly fifteen years beginning with the turn of the 20th century. His first enterprise was a saloon on the corner of Golden Gate Avenue and Market Street (since destroyed).

He became an intermediary between gambling and prostitution merchants and corrupt city government officials. During the first decade of the new century he was considered San Francisco's most powerful underworld figure owning dozens of brothel despite his activities being investigated by a local grand jury.

Bassity arrogantly flaunted his wealth and position by extravagantly sporting diamonds, immaculately tailored and embroidered waistcoats and lavish gifts he gave to prostitutes at *competitor's* brothels.

A brief civic reform movement closed his establishments between 1908-1910. He regained his influence when *his* candidate Patrick McCarthy (who he did fundraising for) was elected mayor in 1910. Bassity was able to get his friend Dan White appointed police chief resulting in honest law enforcement officers transferred to outlying districts. Gambling and prostitution flourished within the Tenderloin.

His resurgence and influence proved brief. When *Sunny Jim* Rolfe was elected mayor in 1912, Bassity's stature faded.

His excessive spending, drunkenness and public debauchery proved his undoing. Always armed, he was renowned for shooting out the lights in brothels and twice arrested for shooting individuals on the street. He was nearly beaten to death on two occasions. His spiraling obesity made him an object of ridicule. In 1917, he was arrested for serving a soldier in his saloon.

He eventually liquidated his San Francisco interests and relocated to Southern California. He spent the bulk of his remaining resources on a failed attempt to purchase a Tijuana racetrack. He was almost bankrupt when he died in 1929.

Diamond Jessie Hayman's Additional Brothels

Dunphy Building: A four-storied brick structure constructed in 1906 features decorative window frames including third level arches, bracket cornice and pediment with Renaissance/Baroque ornamentation. With the destruction of her Ellis Street location, Jessie transferred operations to the top two floors of the newly completed Dunphy Building until the fall of 1907.

Glenwood Parlor House: A three-storied decorative brick structure features rusticated piers, galvanized iron cornice with Renaissance/Baroque ornamentation. Following her Dunphy tenancy, Jessie relocated operations here between 1907 until 1912.

Gotham Lodgings: A four-storied brick structure with rusticated second level. The upper levels feature decorative panels, bands, window surrounds, galvanized iron cornice with Renaissance/Baroque ornamentation. Her final lavish brothel operated from 1912 until her retirement in 1917. The government was cracking down on prostitution establishments based on the perceived health peril for soldiers contracting sexually transmitted diseases. The first floor was leased as a saloon and the second floor was devoted to the parlors and madam's suite. The women's suites, dining room and kitchen were on the upper floors.

Jerome Bassity's Coronado Saloon:
225 Ellis Street, San Francisco

Dunphy Building:
136-142 Taylor Street, San Francisco

The Glenwood Parlor House:
34-48 Mason Street, San Francisco

The Gotham Lodgings:
128-132 Eddy Street, San Francisco

Diane Whipple: Defining Accountability With Vicious Pet Owners

A savage dog mauling that resulted in a young woman's death raised legal, liability and ethical questions as to the extent of human responsibility in raising known vicious pets

Diane Whipple was the victim of a fatal dog attack in San Francisco during January 2001. The dogs were two Presa Canario dogs owned by her third-floor neighbors in the Pacific Heights district of San Francisco.

On January 26, 2001, after returning home with bags of groceries, the monstrous dogs (weighing in excess of 130 pounds) attacked Whipple in the constricted hallway of her apartment building. The two dogs were being kept by her neighbors Marjorie Knoller and husband Robert Noel, both San Francisco attorneys. The dogs were actually owned by two life-sentenced Pelican Bay State prisoners.

The dogs were integral parts of an improbable and illegal dog-fighting business scheme formulated by the prisoner owners. Noel and Knoller had idiotically agreed to take possession of the dogs within their apartment after the dogs proved too violent in a rural environment. Noel and Knoller had originally become acquainted with the prisoners through volunteer legal work. The most bizarre element of this twisted narrative was they had legally adopted one of the prisoners as their son only a few days before the mauling.

The Pacific Heights residence where the dog caretakers and victim lived is an older multi-level Spanish style construction with very narrow hallways. Just prior to the attack, Knoller was taking the dogs up to the roof when they spied and attacked Whipple in the hallway. Whipple had no possibility of escape or defense and suffered a total of 77 wounds to every part of her body except her scalp and bottoms of her feet. She died hours later from her wounds and excessive blood loss.

Both dogs were killed following the attack. In March 2001, a grand jury indicted Knoller and Noel. Knoller was indicted for second-degree murder and involuntary manslaughter. Noel was indicted for involuntary manslaughter. Both faced felony charges of keeping a mischievous dog.

At trial, Knoller argued that she had attempted to defend Whipple during the attack. Her claim was marginalized due to multiple witnesses testifying both caretakers repeatedly refused to control the dogs. The accused pair was villainized by the media as *arrogant* and *unsympathetic figures* for their refusal to even publicly apologize for the attack.

Ultimately, the jury found both Noel and Knoller guilty of involuntary manslaughter and owning a mischievous animal that caused the death of a human being. They found Knoller guilty of second-degree murder. Their convictions were based on the argument that they knew the dogs were aggressive towards other people and that they did not take sufficient precautions.

California suspended their law licenses. Follow-up appeals to the definition of their convictions clouded the final verdict before California appeals courts finally allowing Knoller's second-degree murder conviction to stand. Knoller is currently serving her sentence at the California Institution for Women in Corona following an extended stint at the Valley State Prison for Women in Chowchilla.

Noel was convicted of involuntary manslaughter and after serving a four-year sentence is currently living and working in Solano County. Whipple's domestic partner, Sharon Smith succeeded in suing Knoller and Noel for $1.5 million in civil damages.

The debate continues as to the degree of liability pet owners should be mandated to maintain with known vicious pets.

Diane Whipple's Dog Mauling Death:
2398 Pacific Street, San Francisco

Belle Cora and Donaldina Cameron: Two Chinatown Icons

Belle Cora and Donaldina Cameron's life trajectories couldn't have been more contrasting.

Arabella Ryan, better known as Belle Cora briefly became the leading parlor Madame in San Francisco amidst the California Gold Rush. Although the women never met, their divergent stories originated from buildings located two blocks apart in Chinatown. Both Belle's parlor and Donaldina's Presbyterian House buildings were completely destroyed by the 1906 Earthquake. Donaldina's was reconstructed and remains today, while Belle's establishment permanently perished in the ashes.

Belle Cora was the daughter of a Baltimore minister and reportedly devoted mother. She fell in love with an older man and became pregnant. He vanished. She fled to New Orleans determined to raise the child. The baby died shortly after birth. Belle, alone and devastated, drifted into work at a well-known local brothel.

Dark-haired, voluptuous and stunning, she was renowned for her piercing hazel eyes. She became the house favorite and within a few months was earning more than any prostitute in New Orleans.

She encountered a dapper professional gambler named Charles Cora and together they pursued adventure amidst California's Gold Rush. They left New Orleans via steamship. Upon their arrival in 1849, they began successfully plying their trades in a welcoming and fertile market. In 1850, they opened their first venue in Marysville, quickly followed by another in Sonora.

With these proceeds, in 1852 they opened their third parlor house on Washington Street in the heart of Chinatown. Lavish and opulently decorated, prominent men gravitated towards fine champagne, cuisine and the city's most beautiful woman. Their operation commanded the highest prices. The couple had ascended the height of prosperity, but San Francisco was maturing and hardening towards vice.

As gold fever dissipated by 1855, societal changes were evolving. During the Gold Rush era, the scarcity of women and culture made gambling and prostitution necessary outlets for the influx of male prospectors. In 1854, both were legislated against locally.

An inevitable feud developed between Charles Cora and U.S. Marshal William Richardson that resulted in angry exchanges and threats. The object of the verbal abuse was Belle Cora's reputation. The Richardson couple demanded that the Cora's be ejected from a prominent theatre balcony when they realized they were seated next to each other in the most expensive seats.

The insults continued later in front of the Blue Wing Saloon on Montgomery Street, yards away from the present standing Transamerica Pyramid. In the spirit of western conflict resolution, Charles Cora outdrew Richardson and shot him in the head fatally with his derringer.

Cora was arrested, but represented by the finest local attorney resulting in a hung jury. A local vigilante of 2,000 men stormed the local jailhouse on Broadway Street for a *people's trial* of Cora and another prisoner, Board of Supervisor James Casey. Casey was imprisoned for killing a popular local newspaperman. The sheriff initially refused the mob's demand but promptly reversed his decision when a loaded cannon was pointed at the jail cells.

The trial predictably went against both defendants and they were convicted and sentence to hang. Four days later, Belle married Charles at 11:00 a.m. She assumed his name, but could do little to alter the inevitable. Over 3,000-armed members of a militia secured the execution site at Fort Gunnybags, near the corner of Battery and Sacramento Street. Two hours later, over 8,000 spectators viewed the two men make their final appeals. James Casey proclaimed his innocence in anguish. Cora remained mute.

The two were hung adjacently from the second story windows of Fort Gunnybags. Their deaths symbolically represented a radical reform movement. Belle withdrew in seclusion within her Cora House for over a month utterly distraught. Upon her emergence, she sold the House and began diverting her fortune towards charitable and particularly children's educational programs. Within seven years she would die of unknown causes at the age of 30.

In 1916, a series of articles in the *San Francisco Bulletin* resurrected her controversial legacy. The result was that her body was disinterred from her gravesite at Calvary Cemetery in Colma and laid beside her husband Charles at the Mission Delores cemetery.

Donaldina Cameron was renowned also for her charitable lifestyle, but *throughout* her extended lifespan.

Cameron was revered for her missionary efforts with immigrant Chinese women preventing their exploitation into forced prostitution and indentured servitude. She was a Presbyterian missionary known as *Fahn Quai*, the White Devil as well as the Angry Angel of Chinatown. Born in 1869 seven years following Belle's death, she was raised on a sheep farm in New Zealand before immigrating to California with her Scottish parents at the age of three and a half.

At the age of 23, a family friend introduced Donaldina to the Presbyterian Home in Chinatown where she became employed as a sewing teacher. Her true calling and destiny emerged in 1897 when she became superintendent. The Home was employed as a sanctuary. Housed, fed and protected, the rescued Chinese women would be given an education enabling them to obtain more desirable professions.

Chinatown in the late 19th century was an especially dangerous environment for newly transported women. The Chinese Exclusion Act of 1882, partially intended to prevent sexual trafficking, barred women from entering the United States unless they were already married to a resident. Young women, known as *Mui Tsais* would arrive with forged and false documents indicating they were already members of existing Chinese families. Their illegal status was coined *paper daughters*.

Upon arriving, the women were prey to the ruthless ruling Tongs (secret societies) who sold them as unpaid servants and prostitutes. Their exploited lifestyle was brutal and many survived less than five years under these severe conditions. San Francisco city officials ignored these extreme conditions due to extensive payoffs orchestrated by the Tongs.

Donaldina Cameron proved to be a formidable economic adversary to the Tongs resulting in numerous death threats against her. Advised discreetly of locations housing captive women by their friends or family, she used her cunning, passion and fury to liberate them into her care.

The Chinese women were forced to reside at the Presbyterian Home and were not allowed outside without an escort. They were also obliged to convert to Christianity while they completed their curriculum of English, religion and western housekeeping skills. They were not allowed to leave permanently unless they married a Christian suitor approved by Cameron.

Criticism was sometimes leveled against Donaldina for her failure to integrate Chinese culture into the women's education and her patronizing attitude towards them. Her forced religious conversions and insistence upon absolute control was not universally accepted.

Given the severity of her struggle against powerful forces, abuse and exploitation, compromise was both problematic and impractical. What remains unquestionable is that her courage, faith and heartfelt altruism made her a genuine and inspiring icon.

The 1906 earthquake and fire forced the evacuation of the original Presbyterian Home building. Donaldina returned amidst the flames to retrieve a logbook that detailed her legal guardianship over the girls residing there. This courageous act was to insure none of them might lose their status amidst the chaos that followed the catastrophe.

The original structure was ultimately destroyed, but rebuilt in brick the following year at its current location of 920 Sacramento Street.

Donaldina was responsible for establishing three additional homes for orphaned Chinese children. She wrote extensively, generally to raise financial support for her missions. She retired from her missionary work and the

Presbyterian Home in 1934. The facility was renamed the Donaldina Cameron House in 1942. She died at the age of 98 in 1968. Her efforts were credited with saving and educating over 2,000 Chinese immigrant women.

Her works remain a beacon amidst one of the darkest environments imaginable.

Donaldina Cameron House:
920 Sacramento Street, San Francisco

Fung *Little Pete* Jing Toy: 19th Century Chinatown Gangland Slaying

Within today's narrow and murky alleyways of San Francisco's Chinatown, it is not difficult to imagine a 19th century concentration of opium dens, gambling houses and gangland murders. The 1906 earthquake and fire obliterated most of Chinatown. The majority of buildings and structures were destroyed. Streets, building numbers and the essential identity of the neighborhoods were altered during reconstruction.

One of the subtler but supposedly lasting changes became the declining influence and exodus of the ruling tongs. The tongs evolved out of secret societies founded by revolutionaries in 17th century imperial China. In America, they started during California's Gold Rush, helping immigrants endure the hardships of discrimination. They eventually spread to other parts of the country.

The 19th century tongs tyrannical influence extended into most sectors of Chinatown. Virile leaders emerged and were often displaced violently. No more visible leader represented the era than Fung Jing Toy, more commonly known as *Little Pete*. Pete was known as the dragonhead (the designation of leadership) of the Som Yop Tong. The title is still employed today to crown leaders of the sometimes illicit world of Chinese brotherhoods and gangs.

Little Pete rose to power via old fashion methods. He was considered the best armed, guarded and ruthless of the hatchet men (the then preferred method of execution). His empire included prostitution, gambling and opium sales. Many considered him invincible because of his steel-reinforced hat, chain mail chest protector, German shepherd companions, three bodyguards and twin pistols. He was

76

rumored to have slain over fifty men and amassed a substantial personal fortune. Rising to the summit at 32-years-old, his fate was inevitable. He was as vulnerable as powerful.

Rival tong leaders had placed a $3,000 contract on Pete's life and on January 23, 1897, they found two takers, rumored to be the assassins Lem Jung and Chew Tin Gop. While Little Pete was finishing up a shave without his bodyguards at the Wong Lung barbershop at 819 Washington Street, the duo shoved a .45 caliber revolver under his chain mail and emptied five bullets into his spine. As trained killers, they completed the job with two more into his head.

Little Pete's fixed death stare became the only evidence for the arriving policemen. In the insulated society of Chinese tongs, no one spoke with investigators. No one ever went to public trial nor was convicted. Both assassins later returned to China wealthy men reportedly due to the contract slaying. This was never substantiated.

Today's tenant at the 819 Washington Street address may or may not be occupying the actual site of the fateful barbershop slaying. The re-designation and numbering of buildings following the earthquake created substantial identification chaos.

The tong presence has perhaps never truly vanished or disappeared from contemporary society.

Today, diversely ethnic Asian gangs still operate within Chinatown. The majority maintains discreet public profiles. The gangland past has not been fully buried within the archives. Violent acts such as the 1977 Golden Dragon Restaurant massacre or later contract killings of influential businessman Allen Leung, lawyer Dennis Natali or Vietnamese gang leader Cuong Tran remind outsiders of their clandestine presence.

The rise and swift fall of Fung Jing Toy is repeated regularly in our urban and now suburban environments. The marginalized still feel the need to collectively organize and seize their perceived due share of prosperity, whether legally or illicitly.

**Fung *Little Pete* Jing Toy Killing Site:
819 Washington Street, San Francisco**

The 1977 Golden Dragon Massacre: The Gang Who Didn't Shoot Straight

San Francisco throughout the 1970s was a magnet for racial tension, which sporadically manifested itself into violence. No example proved more spontaneous and deadly than the September 1977 gang related massacre at the Golden Dragon restaurant in Chinatown.

Contemporary Chinese gangs trace their lineage from *tongs*, secret collectives and societies common to southern China. Tongs resemble the clandestine organizational structure of western culture Masonic organizations but are often motivated by more sinister objectives. Their formation initially was influenced by immigrant's needs to band together in combating ethnic exploitation.

Tongs ruthlessly governed Chinatown's criminal activities during the late nineteenth century. Many were disbursed and lost influence following the 1906 earthquake, which obliterated the sector. Some sources insist their presence and influence has never dissipated. Not all tongs are considered disreputable or affiliated with criminal influences. Many of the more established provide essential recognized services such as immigrant counseling, Chinese schools and English classes for adults.

The word *Tong* translates into hall or gathering place. During the late evening of September 3rd, which had spilled into Sunday morning by 2:40 a.m., a hundred Asian and Caucasian diners remained in the popular Golden Dragon restaurant. The Chinese habitually enjoy an *Hsiao Yeh* (little snack). Chinatown restaurants often accommodated these preferences until a traditional closing time of 3:00 a.m. Amongst the Labor Day weekend dining crowd were ten members of the *Wah Ching gang* including their leadership. They were affiliated and sometimes allied with another faction, the *Hop Sing Boys*, whose tong owned the restaurant. Members of the *Hop Sing Boys* were also present that evening.

A rival group, the *Joe Boys* (Chung Ching Yee) was alerted by one of its members, Carlos Jon, who worked at a downtown hotel of their presence. Within a brief span, numerous members of the *Joe Boys* assembled at the home of a Pacifica tattoo artist to launch a surprise assault on their rivals. They distributed firearms including a sawed-off shotgun, conventional shotgun, .45 automatic rifle, .38 handgun, ammunition and nylon stocking masks. They drove to Chinatown in an automobile stolen by gang member Peter Cheung.

Blood had been spilt two months earlier in a gun battle at the Ping Yuen Housing Project between the *Joe Boys* and *Wah Ching*. Four members had been wounded and one killed, 16-year-old *Joe Boys'* member Felix Huey. Retaliation was inevitable and a congested restaurant the ideal opportunity, preventing escape.

The intention behind the attack was to seek out and systematically eliminate the *Wah Ching* members. The plan deviated immediately. Four of the *Joe Boys* randomly sprayed gunfire into the crowded concentration of patrons, employees and tourists. Perhaps the gunmen had panicked anticipating return fire. The shooting spree lasted less than sixty seconds before they fled. The bedlam resulted in five fatalities and eleven wounded.

Not a single *Wah Ching* member was injured. The intended victims were lodged in the rear of the restaurant. Upon sighting the *Joe Boys* entrance and viewing the drawn weapons, they ducked and tipped over their tables for protection, concealing themselves during the fuselage.

Chester Yu had remained in the car and was reported to have driven the group back to Pacifica where they spent the night with other gang members. Another member of the gang and a suspect in the murders, Sai Ying Lee, was never apprehended. His escape from later arrest failed to clarify his exact role in the killings although he was also rumored also to be the getaway driver.

Chester Yu and Tony Szeto were responsible for dumping the employed weapons into the San Francisco Bay near an airport location. The gang members reportedly sawed the guns into bits before dumping them. Yu later escorted police during their investigation to the site where the guns were recovered.

One week later the *Wah Ching* gang would retaliate with the slaying of *Joe Boy Yee* Michael Lee in his Richmond district residence. Mark Chan, another gang member was wounded nine times but miraculous recovered. His gang affiliation resulted in another ambush two years later. He ultimately left San Francisco due to his target status.

One of shooting survivors although not injured, *Hop Sing Boys'* member Raymond *Shrimp Boy* Chow later became one of Chinatown's most notorious gangsters. Once apprehended, he was convicted, imprisoned and a key prosecution witness in the trial against more reputed international crime boss Peter Chong and his tong *Wo Hop To*. His testimony earned him an early release in 2003 and a subsequent reputation as a *reformed* gang member, speaking often and publicly against his former lifestyle.

Not everyone was convinced of his redemption and transformation. Chow was arrested in March 2014 during an FBI raid in connection with an investigation into official corruption by California State Senator Leland Yee. In 2016, Chow was found guilty on 162 counts including racketeering, robbery, aiding and abetting the laundering of drug money and conspiring to deal in the illegal sales of goods. For these crimes and arranging the 2005 execution style slaying of Allen Leung, a prominent Chinatown businessman, he was sentenced to life in prison. He is currently serving his term at the United States Penitentiary in Terre Haute, Indiana.

The five innocent fatalities from the Golden Dragon shootings included Denise Louie (20s), Calvin Fong (18), Paul Wada (25), Donald Quan (20) and Fong Wang (48), a Taiwanese waiter at the restaurant.

The *Joe Boys* gang ultimately disbanded. Four confirmed shooters were eventually arrested and convicted for the massacre. Additional gang members were convicted for accomplice roles and given reduced sentences based on their cooperation with investigators.

The shooters included:

Tom Yu, the attributed leader of the attack, was convicted of five counts of first-degree murder, 11 counts of assault and one count of conspiracy to commit murder. He appealed his conviction all the way to the United States Supreme Court. He was paroled from the California State Prison in Vacaville in 2015.

Peter Ng was convicted of five counts of first-degree murder and 11 counts of assault. He is no longer listed on the California prison rolls under this name and presumably has been released.

Melvin Yu was convicted of five counts of first-degree murder and 11 counts of assault. In 1995, a Los Angeles Times article profiled his incarceration at the Deuel Vocational Institution in Tracy. He is no longer listed on the California prison rolls under this name and presumably has been released.

Curtis Tam, also known as Stuart Lin, claimed to have accompanied the shooters under duress and aimed his shotgun away from diners. He was an immigrant from Hong Kong who was then 18 and attending Galileo High School. He was the first arrest in the case. He was convicted on five counts of second-degree murder and 11 counts of assault. He was released in October 1991.

The accomplices:

Chester Yu served two years in the California Youth Authority at Stockton. He was released in 1980 and moved out of California.

Carlos Jan, who placed the original call informing the gang of the Wah Chin's presence was given immunity for his testimony against Tom Yu and relocated out of California.

Peter Chung, who'd stolen the car used to transport the gang from Pacifica cooperated fully with the police investigation and testified in several of the trials. He served less than one year at the California Youth Authority at Stockton. In 1980, a passing truck accidentally sideswiped him at night as he sought help on foot for his disabled vehicle on Interstate 580.

Tony Szeto was convicted for two years in state prison for his assistance in dumping the murder weapons. California's first appellate court reversed the conviction due to insufficient corroboration. The prosecution team was successful in reinstating the conviction before the California Supreme Court. That decision became a leading precedent case for laws involving accomplice corroboration.

Writer Brockman Morris in his book *Bamboo Tigers* was a major source in relating the fates of many of these participants. His most ironic portrayal was the one written about Gan Wah Robert Woo. Woo received a $100,000 reward offered by the City of San Francisco for his information leading to the apprehension, arrest and conviction of the perpetrators. He had reportedly declined to participate in the killings but knew intimate details about them, which he revealed to investigators. A career criminal, he was detained at various facilities throughout his life and became a visible target once his role as star informant was revealed.

He ultimately relocated to New York where he planned to resettle and marry. In 1983 he abruptly vanished. He resurfaced and was shot fatally by police during a botched December 20, 1984 gang heist of the Jin Hing jewelry store in Los Angeles' Chinatown.

The paradox behind the involved parties was that each were young, physically slight, barely spoke English and recklessly impulsive in their preparations and ultimate execution of their plan. Despite their age, they were hardened killers and criminals already involved in stolen property, extortion and illegal drug trade.

The Golden Dragon restaurant, despite the carnage, continued operations the same evening of the shootings with notable damage. In 1981, the Golden Dragon and its owners Jack Lee, B. Hong Ng and the Hop Sing Tong paid a reported $450,000 out of court settlement to two wounded survivors and families of the three of the murder victims. The restaurant continued in business until 2006 but ultimately closed after a failed health inspection and failure to pay their employees for numerous months.

The Imperial Palace restaurant has since resumed operations in the popular location.

The San Francisco police department established the *Asian Gang Task Force* following the massacre. The killings had been preceded by a reported thirty-nine murders during the decade by drive-by shootings and assassinations. The task force today has been credited with having contained many potentially explosive situations but their presence is incapable of restricting society's transformation.

Tong societies remain active in Chinatown. The legend of the reticent Chinese wall of silence remains intact. Southeastern Asian gangs within San Francisco have proliferated. The Imperial Palace restaurant now closes promptly at 9:30 p.m. nightly.

**Golden Dragon Restaurant Shooting Site:
818 Washington Street, San Francisco**

The Golden Gate Bridge: An Attractive Suicide Magnet

On August 7, 1937, World War I veteran Harold B. Wobber disembarked from a bus turnstile leading to the freshly completed Golden Gate Bridge. Wobber, a descendant from a California pioneer family strolled the length of the bridge towards Marin County with a companion he'd just met. Halfway back on their return, he handed the companion his coat, scaled the railing and plunged 260 feet to his death. His body was never recovered.

When the Golden Gate Bridge was completed in late May, the 1.7 mile long span was the longest suspension main bridge in the world. The engineering masterpiece was and remains one of the most picturesque and aesthetic crossings in the world. Eleven men perished during the construction, ten during a single day. Wobber was the first recorded suicide.

Harold Wobber had suffered shell shock during his tour of duty in France from 1917 to 1918. He abandoned his post-war job running a lunchroom on the Oakland waterfront in 1930 then checked into a veteran's hospital. He remained there seven years during which his wife divorced him and he may have been subjected to electric shock therapy.

The suicide total has been estimated at approximately 1,700 following over eighty years of operation. The span has become the second-most popular suicide spot globally, outranked by China's Nanjing Yangtze Bridge.

The most famous jumpers have included five-year-old Marilyn DeMont and her father in 1945, Marc Salinger (the son of President Kennedy's Press Secretary Pierre Salinger) in 1977, and Roy Raymond, the founder of women's lingerie chain Victoria's Secret in 1993. The exact number of victims is impossible to calculate, since many have jumped unseen, in the darkness or their bodies have never been recovered.

The four-second fall at 75 miles per hour is the equivalent of a speeding truck smashing against a concrete building. The survival rate is estimated at less than 2%, but is probably even lower. It is estimated that 5% of the jumpers survive the initial impact but generally drown or die of hypothermia in the frigid waters. Less than forty identified individuals have survived the impact. All have suffered crippling injuries. Thousands have been talked down from their intended jumps. Installation of steel siding prevention netting has begun. Completion is scheduled for 2022.

Two cables that pass through the primary dual towers are fixed in concrete at each end to support the weight of the roadway. Each cable is composed of 27,572 strands of wire accounting for 80,000 miles of wire in the main cables. The bridge has over 1.2 million steel rivets. Average daily traffic is approximately 110,000 vehicles.

Joseph Strauss was the chief engineer in charge of the overall design. The final suspension design was credited to Leon Moisseiff, also the engineer of New York City's Manhattan Bridge. The Art Deco design was credited to Alfred Finnila.

These three principal designers and innovators certainly had little suspicion what their aesthetic masterpiece would ultimately symbolize to future generations of unhappy and desperate individuals.

In the chilling words of survivor Ken Baldwin, *I just wanted to disappear*. At 28, the instant he leapt to an almost certain death, he realized, *The moment I saw my hands leave the railing, I knew I wanted to live*.

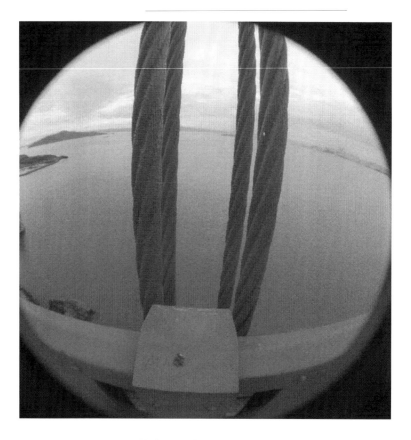

Golden Gate Bridge:
Golden Gate Straits connecting San Francisco with
Marin County

Jeff Adachi: The Double Life and Death of San Francisco's Public Defender

The secret double life of 59-year-old San Francisco Public Defender Jeff Adachi resolutely collapsed as he expired inside a Telegraph Hill apartment on the evening of February 22, 2019. Paramedics arrived to discover Adachi unresponsive from an apparent fatal heart attack.

The narrative might have closed at that point. Jeff Adachi had a history of heart disease and a fatal coronary might have been considered simply tragic, but not entirely unforeseen. The story however became gamier.

As intimate details of Adachi's final day and hours began to emerge publicly along with the results from his autopsy, the flames of scandal were fanned.

The location of Adachi's death was an apartment lent to him by a real estate agent friend for a couple of days. Adachi was married, but the loan wasn't employed for a romantic getaway with his wife. Instead, he awoke his final morning with a woman reportedly named *Caterina*. The pair spent the day together that included a late breakfast followed in the afternoon by cannabis edibles.

They dined together at a North Beach restaurant and consumed a complete meal including champagne and/or wine. As the meal progressed, Adachi complained of upper abdominal pain and began sweating profusely. The symptoms were the early stages of cardiac arrest. Had he been hospitalized immediately, he might have survived.

Instead the couple returned to the Telegraph Hill apartment where Adachi's agony continued despite lying down and swallowing an ibuprofen. Caterina asked if he wished to visit a hospital, but he declined erroneously thinking it might be simply heartburn. In her version of events, he sent her to a corner store to purchase over the counter stomach medication.

She returned. His condition had worsened and he appeared disoriented and confused. Sensing the severity of the situation, she telephoned 911. During the call, she was instructed to perform CPR. By the time the ambulance arrived, she had vanished. Adachi was declared dead upon arrival at the hospital.

The later toxicology report conducted by San Francisco's Medical Examiner confirmed the anticipated alcohol intake, but also traces of cocaine and benzodiazepines in his system. The autopsy acknowledged his significant coronary artery disease and fibrosis. His health complications may have killed him eventually, but doubtlessly under entirely different circumstances.

Attorneys representing the Adachi family six months later released reports from three independent forensics experts disputing the findings of the San Francisco Medical Examiner's office. They argued the cause of death should have simply been stated as *natural causes*. Their perspective is understandable because traces of cocaine found in Adachi's system would raise important ethical and embarrassing questions as to his legal suitability to perform his professional duties.

Adachi was raised middle class in Sacramento. His parents and grandparents spent part of World War II in a Japanese internment camp. He graduated from UC Berkeley and earned his law degree from the Hastings College of Law in 1985.

His professional trajectory had been subject to the tumultuous winds of politics, but he had emerged as the solely elected Public Defender in California. He was re-elected twice unopposed. His ambitions and interests were diversified including sponsoring a ballot amendment oriented towards pension reform and a 2011 run for Mayor. He finished sixth from a field of sixteen candidates. He wrote, produced and directed documentary films.

At his funeral, he was widely lauded for his professional contributions, talent and career as an ethnic pioneer. The details regarding his duplicity and the unexplained circumstances behind his death remained unwelcome speculation.

One of the most controversial aspects regarding the detailed public disclosure was who was responsible for the news media leaks? Journalist Bryan Carmody's security front door was pried open and home searched in an attempt to discover the his information sources. Carmody had obtained embarrassing documentation behind Adachi's death and sold the information to news outlets. The police raid conducted with a search warrant *borrowed* Carmody's cameras, computers, cellphones and professional notes.

The police application for a warrant neglected to state that Carmody was a professional journalist and protected under California's Shield Law. In court, a judge invalidated the search warrant due to this omission. San Francisco's police chief William Scott publicly apologized to Carmody and admitted his investigators had *made mistakes*.

The lesson behind Adachi's death and botched concealment once again raises the eternal question regarding the lives of public figures. Is the public entitled to know about the private indiscretions of elected officials? Did Jeff Adachi compromise his professional integrity by living a double life?

Jeff Adachi's Death Site:
46 Telegraph Place, San Francisco

Joseph *The Animal* Barboza: The Inevitability of a Lifestyle Path

The longevity prospects of an East Coast Mafia hitman and informer would not appear substantial. When such an individual, under the U.S. government witness protection program returns to his previous profession and risky lifestyle, his prospects diminish into an inevitable death sentence.

The killing of Joseph *The Animal* Barboza surprised no one. The San Francisco location of the contract slaying was unusual and the source of his betrayal, an evident surprise to the victim.

Barboza was a confirmed New England mobster and feared hitman whose life did nothing to further the advancement of humanity. Acknowledged appropriately by his long-term legal council, F. Lee Bailey, the news of his assassination brought the quip *no great loss to society*.

An individual such a Barboza cultivates many associates of unsavory nature and few friends amongst the cesspool they inhabit during their lifetime. His background and criminal exploits make intriguing but repulsive viewing even to those sharing a fascination with the mobster lifestyle. The ultimate betrayal by an associate, inflated self-promotion and later return to criminal activity in Northern California contributed towards his predictable outcome.

Barboza's most noteworthy distinction was assuming the role of FBI informant and becoming one of the initial participants in the Federal Witness Protection Program. His testimony proved influential in securing convictions against several organized crime figures. A fresh identity and vocational occupation however could not alter his

97

sociopathic tendencies. When one has spent an entire lifetime cultivating influential enemies, violent death becomes simply a question of where, when and in what manner.

The litany of death attributed to Barboza may have exceeded double digits on both coasts. Exact numbers are difficult to quantify from imaginative boasting and speculation. A proficient hitman rarely acknowledges his handiwork as someday he may face accountability.

An individual such as Joseph Barboza who acquired a nickname The Animal is clearly respected but doubtlessly psychotic. His second-degree conviction for the killing of a man in 1971 in Santa Rosa exposed his actual identity while he was on trial. He served a marginal five years in Folsom prison for the murder, but his fate was sealed. Out on parole in October 1975, Barboza was targeted for revenge.

His February 11, 1976 death was a classic set-up and pristine assassination arranged in conjunction with one of Barboza's friends. Following lunch at his friend's residence in his San Francisco Sunset District neighborhood, Barboza returned to his parked car adjacent to the house. He was armed with a Colt .38 but ambushed at close range by four shotgun blasts before he could respond.

Reportedly defiant to the end, Barboza shouted obscenities at his killers as they sped away. He died immediately afterwards.

There were no eyewitnesses. The killing site and neighborhood today is serene and nearly deserted during daylight. No one has ever been charged with his death. The responsible party(s) has been rumored to be another mob hitman. The investigation remains open but with minimal enthusiasm towards resolution.

Joe *The Animal* Barboza's death became simply another combat casualty in the warfare between society and organized crime. Morals may be drawn from his sordid life and demise. They tend to be dismissed with the public's continuing fascination with cult criminal personalities. Barboza's contribution to the campaign is largely forgotten.

There remained then and now numerous candidates to supplant him. Compliance and acceptance of society's regulations make uneventful television and motion picture viewing.

PHOTOS: Sunset District house, Adjacent sidewalk where Barboza was shot

Joseph *The Animal* Barboza Contract Killing:

Sidewalk adjacent to 1700 25th Avenue, San Francisco

Kevin Collins: A Solitary Bus Bench Memorial to Every Parent's Nightmare

On February 10, 1984, Kevin Collins, aged ten, left a basketball practice early from his school's gymnasium. Shortly after 7:55 p.m. Kevin was last seen sitting on a San Francisco bus bench at the corner of Oak Street and Masonic Avenue. During February, evenings turn dark around 6 p.m. He vanished into the shadows and was never seen or located again.

Child abductions even then were not novel but typically localized. Kevin's disappearance became national news. His story inspired an unprecedented massive search including the nationwide distribution of flyers, a cover story in a national magazine, his photo image on milk cartons and pleas for his return from local politicians. His body was never found. His disappearance represented a turning point in abduction awareness as these responses later became commonplace.

For twelve years, Kevin's father David operated a search center in an effort to find his son. The strain of Kevin's disappearance and follow-up search efforts shattered his marriage. Despite his efforts and the nationwide coordinated hunt, no solid suspect has ever emerged.

The only positive consequences from the tragedy have been heightened national interest towards the plight of missing children. Law enforcement officials have also learned how to better coordinate their response to child abductions.

An isolated bus park bench remains embedded at the corner of Oak Street and Masonic Avenue. It is the sole reminder of a boy who disappeared without the slightest trace. Daily commuters, transfer riders and local transients have little idea of the grief it once symbolized to a broken family and its historical local significance.

Kevin Collins Abduction:
Last Sighting: Bus Stop Bench, Oak and Masonic
Streets, San Francisco

Maiden Lane: Where Once Not a Fair Maiden Was to be Seen

In 1872, St. Mark's Place was changed to Morton Street. The two-block stretch of roadway began at Kearny Street and ended at Stockton Street. This concentration of vice was notorious for gambling, prostitution, assaults and muggings. It wasn't uncommon for a brothel patron to lose not only his fee for services rendered, but all money and valuables he foolishly carried into the parlor. The slang for bordello on Morton Street was *bawdy houses* and *bagnios*.

Gambling was rampant in saloons and brothels. The most common con game was *bunko* and the *panel game*. Victims often refused to file charges for fear of their name being associated with the neighborhood.

In 1872, a petition with sixty Morton Street resident signatures was submitted to Police Chief Crowley requesting the suppression of nine houses of prostitution. The petition detailed the *danger and annoyance created by the idle and dissolute men who congregate in the vicinity. Respectable women cannot go into the street without danger of insult by the hoodlums*.

The following day, Crowley ordered a police blockage on several of the more notorious Morton Street houses. The blockage had only a marginal effect on the prostitution trade. A seesaw battle continued over the next decade with police going undercover. Their efforts were often undermined by payoffs to top law enforcement officials and one Police Commissioner, Matthew Collins.

Collins was put on trial for allegedly being viewed taking a bribe through a door containing three strategically drilled holes from courtesan Maggie Kennedy at 129 Morton

Street. During the trial, the other Commissioners were anxious to examine the door to verify that it matched the account. Officer Rainsbury and a carpenter named Roberson were dispatched to the address to retrieve the door. Distracted by a woman (probably a house employee) the detective and carpenter were duped long enough for the door to mysteriously disappear. Regardless, Matthew Collins was dismissed from the force *for receiving a bribe from a Morton Street woman of ill-repute*. The elusive three-holed door was never recovered.

For police, patrolling the neighborhood could be hazardous. In a July 1879 newspaper article, four men ascended upon an officer attending to a reported robbery in the district. Following an assault, he emptied four cartridges towards his assailants. His shots missed naturally. One week later, one of the assailants was arrested in Oakland.

Throughout the 1880s, the street remained dangerous and its poor reputation remained in the headlines. It was reported that the street was finally cleansed of prostitution in 1896. The 1906 Earthquake and fire completed the eradication by decimating the entire street.

In 1898, the avenue was renamed Union Square Street based on its reformed reputation. In 1904, it was changed again to Manila Street before returning back once again to Union Square Street in 1921. In 1922, a local jeweler petitioned to have the name replaced with Maiden Lane in honor of an identically named street in Manhattan. The name has endured and hinged white gates symbolically open into a pedestrian exclusive mall. The contemporary version features high-end boutiques, art galleries and the V.C. Morris Gift shop designed by famed architect Frank Lloyd Wright.

Maiden Lane, San Francisco

Mary Ellen Pleasant: A Civil Rights Pioneer With a Lengthy Shadow

Mary Ellen Pleasant was literally one of San Francisco's most colorful yet sublime personalities of the late 19th century.

Helen Holdredge's biography *Mammy Pleasant* written in 1953 vilified Pleasant, yet Mary Ellen still emerged as a forceful and mythical character. Holdredge's fanciful writing emphasized Pleasant's involvement with black magic, mysticism and extreme manipulative tactics to attain her objectives. The author implied that Pleasant was directly responsible for the death of her business partner and rumored lover Thomas Bell, a renowned banker and proprietor of the mysterious Bell Mansion located at 1661 Octavia Street in San Francisco.

Author Holdredge's sources were predominately diaries she had acquired from Teresa Bell, Thomas' estranged wife from a marriage Pleasant had arranged. Theresa Bell was later institutionalized and had a major falling out with her mentor Pleasant.

Mary Ellen Pleasant was a Creole born entrepreneur and financial speculator. During that era, these depictions did not exist for members of her race or gender. Light-skinned, she could pass for Caucasian and was officially known for running exclusive men's eating establishments. Her exposure to insider investment information at her lavishly catered meals enabled her and Bell, initially a clerk with the Bank of California, to amass a substantial fortune in excess of $30 million.

Mary Ellen's life however was far more expansive and impressive than simply financial trading. She worked on the Underground Railroad across many states and helped bring it to California during the Gold Rush era. She was a friend and financial supporter of John Brown and well recognized within abolitionist circles.

After the Civil War, Pleasant publicly changed her racial designation from *White* to *Black* in the city directory. She further began a series of court battles to fight laws prohibiting blacks from riding trolleys and other such abuses. In 1866, she successfully sued and won money damages against two separate railroad companies for racial discrimination when she and two other women of color were ejected from local streetcars.

She became the conduit for the African-American community within San Francisco. The majority of job placements, arranged marriages and favors were coordinated through her. This actual and implied power stirred up resentment and inevitable gossip.

The 30-room Thomas Bell mansion, constructed in 1879, was designed and furnished by Pleasant who managed the household and the all of the Bell couple's arrangements. This control and orchestration included all financial, entertainment, clothing, employment and even social agenda decisions. Throughout this period she maintained a low profile and was frequently dismissed as merely a housekeeper. Pleasant rarely socialized within Caucasian circles but everyone knew *Mammy* Pleasant, a designation she despised.

The Bell's lived separate lives and Pleasant served as their mediator. Rumors of voodoo, blackmail, prostitution and even trafficking infants were circulated about the operations of the manor. Given the remote geographical distance from downtown, such gossip wasn't surprising.

On the late evening of October 15, 1892, Thomas Bell mysteriously fell to his death from the top of a staircase twenty feet to the basement. Only Pleasant and Fred Bell, his eldest son were home. Speculation abounded that Bell had been drugged with mulled wine and pushed to his demise.

Naturally, Mary Ellen Pleasant was the prime subject and has remained so for over a century later.

The coroner ruled the death accidental. Bell had apparently been ill for the prior two months. There was accepted speculation that he may have woken up disoriented and simply fallen. Teresa Bell in her diaries thought otherwise. She elaborated on a gruesome tale that Pleasant had hastened Bell's death an hour after the fall by probing into an open skull wound with her index finger. No one has been able to confirm or conclusively dispute the imaginative account, particularly the author.

Later in life, a series of court battles with Sarah Althea Hill, Senator William Sharon, and Teresa Bell damaged Pleasant's reputation and cost her resources and wealth. Pleasant died in San Francisco on January 4, 1904 in poverty and was buried in the Tulocay Cemetery in Napa.

Sorting out fact and rumor has proven impossible. The 30-room Octavia Street mansion burned down in 1925 and was replaced in 1927 by Green's Eye Hospital. Six remaining eucalyptus trees that Pleasant planted and a historical marker have been designated by the city of San Francisco as Mary Ellen Pleasant Memorial Park.

The truth about Mary Ellen Pleasant remains as elusive and enigmatic as the woman herself.

**Mary Ellen Pleasant's Former Mansion Location:
1661 Octavia Street, San Francisco**

Miles Archer: San Francisco's Only Murder Site Commemorative

Burrit Street is a small alleyway flaring off from Bush Street in downtown San Francisco. Prominently mounted is a plaque that could easily be mistaken for a notation of historical importance. Ironically, it is the sole commemorative marker in the city of a murder site.

The plaque reads, *On Approximately This Spot, Miles Archer, Partner Of Sam Spade, Was Done In By Brigid O'Shaughnessy*. Of course Miles Archer, Sam Spade and even Brigid O'Shaughnessy are not historical characters. They were fictionally invented by author Dashiell Hammett for the book and film, *The Maltese Falcon*.

This alleyway is only a few blocks away from Hammett's actual apartment at 891 Post Street, Apartment #401. Since Hammett habitually blurred reality into fiction, it is of little surprise that Sam Spade coincidentally lived there too.

**Miles Archer Murder Plaque:
Burrit Street, San Francisco**

Warren Gamaliel Harding: The Poisoning of a President?

The Presidential Suite of San Francisco's Palace Hotel, Room #888 requires significant financial substance to reserve. Unassumingly positioned amidst the eighth-floor opulence, its role in American history is often forgotten.

The Presidential Suite was the death site of 29th American President Warren Harding under mysterious circumstances. Harding coined the memorable quotation: *I have no trouble with my enemies. I can take care of my enemies in a fight. But my friends, my goddamned friends, they're the ones who keep me walking the floors at nights!*

Amidst more innocent times and media absence, Harding's phrasing became one of his few memorable utterances during an unremarkable presidency. Perhaps he should have taken more care looking over his immediate shoulder with regard to his personal affairs.

Scarcely known, the Republication Party chose Harding, an Ohio Senator, as an inoffensive candidate during their hopelessly deadlocked 1920 convention. Following World War I, two terms by then incapacitated Democrat Woodrow Wilson and a strong minority progressive movement within the Party, Harding became the best compromise for the Republican conservative wing. American voters agreed, electing him by a significant margin of 60% to 34% over Democratic Ohio newspaper publisher James M. Cox.

His campaign slogan of a *return to normalcy* after the fatigue of global warfare was popular amongst voters seeking isolationism and a stronger internal economic focus. This philosophy ultimately ushered in seven years of prosperity, rampant financial speculation and accompanying corruption.

Harding lavishly showered his friends, contributors and associates with powerful government positions. They rewarded his fidelity with previously unimaginable levels of graft and corruption. The most sensation political disgrace of the era, the infamous Teapot Dome Scandal forever tainted him.

Barring John F. Kennedy, Harding cultivated the most prolific Presidential reputation as an obsessive womanizer and philanderer, but only after his death. The accusations were published his detractors posthumously. He was rumored and alleged to have had extramarital affairs and sexual encounters with numerous women. One writer, Nan Britton, a 22-year old campaign volunteer, thirty years his junior, claimed in her 1927 book, *The President's Daughter*, that Harding had in fact fathered her daughter. Published DNA results testing in 2015 confirmed his paternity.

Other reports of trysts surfaced including some within the confines of the White House under the guard of U.S. Secret Service agents. Unsubstantiated claims of orgies, counter claims of Harding's sterility and troves of discovered intimate letters fueled a myriad of conjectures. None shed even minimal insight into a man many observers claimed was pathetically shy, especially around women.

Following stints as a teacher, insurance agent, and lawyer, Harding established his reputation as a newspaper publisher before his successful entry into politics. In 1891, he married Florence Kling DeWolfe, the daughter of his newspaper rival Amos Kling DeWolfe. She was a divorcee, five years Harding's senior and the mother of a young son.

She reportedly pursued Harding until he reluctantly proposed. Her acute business sense, social standing and ambition made the marriage a preview model of noteworthy political liaisons to follow. She was reputed to have maintained a red book filled with notations about individuals who had offended her.

Florence Harding was clearly not a woman to be trifled with nor publicly humiliated.

The workings of the federal government and the geographical location of Washington D.C. in 1923 was isolated from the western United States. Transcontinental airline travel, radio and television were nonexistent. In June of 1923, Harding launched an ambitious westward cross-country *Voyage of Understanding* to connect with Americans and elaborate through public speaking and informal talks, his political agenda and policies. During this trip, he became the first President to visit the Alaskan territories and Canada when he toured Vancouver, British Columbia.

Rumors of his declining health had persisted since the fall of 1922 with speculation that he was suffering from chronic exhaustion and coronary disease. The stress behind the rampant corruption within his administration and possibly his marital infidelities had radically affected his sleeping patterns and recuperative powers.

Harding's tour following Vancouver traveled by train through Seattle to Portland. He canceled his speech in Portland and his train continued to San Francisco where he checked into the Palace Hotel Suite, then numbered 8064. En route, Secretary of Commerce Herbert Hoover wired his personal friend Dr. Ray Wilbur to meet, examine and personally evaluate the President.

At the Palace, Harding, severely exhausted, was diagnosed with a respiratory illness believed to be pneumonia. He was given digitalis and caffeine that apparently helped relieve his heart condition and sleeplessness.

On Thursday evening, August 2nd, Harding's health had appeared to improve. His pulse was normal and lung infection subsided. This apparent recovery enabled his presiding doctors the luxury of leaving him unattended while they dined together.

The account of this subsequent period was the basis for fueling later speculation and controversy. Unexpectedly during their absence, Harding shuddered and died in the middle of a conversation with his wife. Some accounts have her reading by his side a previous weeks article from the influential Saturday Evening Post about him entitled *A Calm View of a Calm M*an. At 7:35 p.m. he was pronounced dead and the national news wires reported the event fifteen minutes later.

The majority of attending doctor's examinations concluded that Harding had died of congestive heart failure. One, Dr. Sawyer, a homeopathic friend of the Harding family suggested he had succumbed to a fatal stroke. Consensus was mixed and an official press release stated the cause of death was some *brain evolvement*, probably an apoplexy. Many close observers to Harding would have argued that throughout his professional career, his inflexibility and limited thinking capabilities would have inhibited any significant brain evolvement.

What immediately followed his death would seem inconceivable with today's social media frenzy and disclosure-obsessed society. Mrs. Harding refused to allow an autopsy and her request was respected. This evasiveness in determining an exact cause of death and his abrupt demise before only a single witness aroused immediate questions. Certain questionable sources suggested that poisoning by a jealous, embarrassed and vengeful spouse artificially prompted his death. Suicide was also speculated. Both theories have been essentially discounted over the years due to Harding's documented medical condition preceding his death.

His political reputation proved so damaged from the scandals, his sudden death only intensified unanswered questions involving both his knowledge and involvement in the illegalities. Florence Harding donated less than 20% of his personal papers for posterity due to his fractured reputation. Subsequent President Herbert Hoover in 1931 categorized the Harding legacy as one of *tragic betrayal*, absolving the man of intimate insider knowledge or direct participation. History however does not always sustain nor validate a single individual's opinion.

Speculation remains a popular American pastime, particularly when multiple potential motives exist for murder. Infidelity and mediocrity stimulate conjecture and the imagination. Only Florence Harding knew for certain what happened during their time alone on the fateful evening of August 2nd.

A four-day eastward procession returned Harding's casket to the East Room of the White House pending a state funeral. Millions lined the tracks in cities and towns to pay their respects and mourn an individual they had minimal prior contact with. Published reports at the time indicated he was genuinely liked and admired despite his leadership failings.

Calvin Coolidge succeeded Harding. His low profile, stoic and aloof personality reflected his administration's governing policy. His policies (or lack of them) were ultimately blamed for enabling business abuses due to almost nonexistent government regulation.

Coolidge became the first President to ultimately integrate the emerging media of radio into his public communications. *Silent Cal's* personality and bland delivery failed to arouse passion with the American public. Satirist writer Dorothy Parker upon being informed that Coolidge had died, famously remarked, *How can they tell?*

Many attribute the casual and negligent policies of the Harding and Coolidge administrations for sowing the seeds of the 1927 stock market collapse and ensuing Great Depression. Their successor, Herbert Hoover inherited the impending catastrophe and its repercussions dominated his legacy.

Hoover was an eminently more competent businessman and administrator than his two predecessors. The accumulated malaise from rampant financial speculation and world economic stagnation however proved overwhelming for his leadership capabilities.

Warren Harding's popularity has historically stagnated in comparison to the varying fluctuations of his contemporaries. This indifference towards his legacy has made the demand for concrete explanations behind his death marginal. Adventurous guests and visitors to the hotel do not have access to the suite but may view an oversized scrapbook maintained by the hotel regarding Harding's ill-fated stay.

The cost for immediate and direct communication with his departed spirit is exorbitant. The room rate reportedly exceeds $3000 per night and remains unpublished on the hotel's website.

Cohabitation with posterity, no matter how morbid, does not come cheaply.

Palace Hotel Room #888:
2 New Montgomery Street, San Francisco

Jim Jones and the Peoples Temple Massacre: No Way Home

Writer Thomas Wolfe's novel *You Can't Go Home Again* aptly summarized the plight of Peoples Temple members isolated in the jungle of Jonestown, Guyana in 1978. Most of the resident cult's followers had long ago abandoned their own birth families to follow a charismatic orator, the Reverend Jim Jones

For the dispossessed, the marginalized and the forgotten who had abandoned the San Francisco Bay area and relocated to this isolated outpost, a single instruction remained on November 18, 1978. They were commanded to drink a concoction of cyanide-laced, grape-flavored Kool-Aid or face immediate shotgun execution. Each complied.

The resulting mass suicides and killings resulted in 918 deaths including 276 children. Among the victims were US Congressman Leo Ryan whose visit and investigation into the encampment triggered the fatal sequence of events. Jones' security personnel gunned down Ryan and his entourage as they attempted to depart via a nearby airstrip at Port Kaituma. In retrospect, the climatic slaughter should have seemed inevitable given the numerous advance-warning signals.

The Peoples Temple was an organization founded in 1955 by Jim Jones under the guise of a structured religion. By the mid-1970s, the Temple possessed over a dozen locations in California. The headquarters were based in San Francisco. The origins of the movement began in Indianapolis, Indiana inspired by Jones fascination with communism. Jones masqueraded his preaching under as social gospel virtues primarily out of fear of reprisals for his communist leanings.

Borrowing tactics such as clairvoyant revelations, healing tricks and fiery rhetoric from Pentecostal movements, the Peoples Temple expanded. The movement attracted diverse classes of people enabling them to generate income and accomplish Jones' social agenda. Jones and Temple members knowingly faked healings because they discovered as a result, donations increased. These healings involved chicken livers and other animal tissue, claimed by Jones (and confederate Temple members) to be cancerous tissues removed from the body.

Two essential differences separated Jones' operations from comparative cults; the composition of his congregation and his savvy political activism.

The Peoples Temple earned a reputation for aiding the cities' poorest citizens, especially racial minorities, drug addicts, and the homeless. The Temple made strong connections with the California state welfare system. During the 1970s, the Peoples Temple owned and ran at least nine residential care homes for the elderly, six homes for foster children, and a state-licensed 40-acre ranch for developmentally disabled persons. The Temple elite handled members' insurance claims and legal problems, effectively acting as a client-advocacy group.

The Temple further distinguished itself from most religious movements with its overtly political message. It combined Jones' political sympathies with the reality that he could help turn out large numbers of volunteers and votes to gain the support of a number of prominent politicians. Jones' ability to mobilize large numbers of his members within short notice ingratiated him with San Francisco's political elite including Mayor George Moscone, Governor Jerry

Brown, Lieutenant Governor Mervyn Dymally, Assemblyman Willie Brown (later Mayor), Harvey Milk, District Attorney Joseph Freitas, State Senator Milton Marks and future Mayor Art Agnos. San Francisco's most visible voice at the San Francisco Chronicle, columnist Herb Caen regularly wrote favorably of Jim Jones in print.

Incredibly, their associations with Jones while he was headquartered in San Francisco barely tarnished their own political legacies despite the Guyana tragedy.

Each evaded close scrutiny, especially Moscone, who staunchly refused investigating the Peoples Temple operations despite repeated requests. Following a narrow election victory in 1975 where Jones' labor resources proved invaluable, Moscone had appointed Jones as Chairman of the San Francisco Housing Authority Commission.

Political obligations to Jones ultimately proved profoundly deeper than any moral concern towards the welfare of his followers. Political debts were owed to Jones and their silence and nonintervention was repayment. Moscone and Milk would be assassinated ten days following the massacre.

In 1974, the Peoples Temple signed a lease to rent land in Guyana. The community created on this property was called the Peoples Temple Agricultural Project, or informally, Jonestown. It had as few as 50 residents in early 1977. Jones saw Jonestown as both a socialist paradise and a sanctuary from media scrutiny.

The Temple's growing political influence and higher local visibility opened the organization up to media inquiry from sources within and outside of San Francisco. An

123

investigative article on their operations was written by Marshall Kilduff and published by *New West Magazine* containing numerous allegations of fraud, assault and potential kidnapping. Subsequent media articles would follow raising a disturbing profile of the Temple's activities and operations.

The exodus to Guyana by Jones' followers required several weeks of preparation and bureaucratic passport formalities. It was reported that Jones himself fled to Guyana the very evening that the contents of Kilduff's *New West* article (yet to be published) was read to him over the phone.

The Temple's pattern of control, beatings and abuse continued upon the their arrival en mass in Jonestown, removed from investigating eyes. Ultimately Congressman Ryan's visit sealed his and the colony's fate. Jones determined that Ryan could not be allowed to return to California with what he had observed and witnessed firsthand.

Today Jim Jones is a conveniently discarded memory. His cult of personality has been forever tarnished. His former political allies have distanced themselves from the man and the movement. The San Francisco Peoples Temple building has become resurrected into a post office station on Geary Street.

The memories of the forgotten and dispossessed Jonestown residents remain so. 412 unclaimed bodies from the Guyana mass suicide are buried at the Evergreen Cemetery in Oakland. Jim Jones name is inscribed on one of the four marble tombstones with no reference to his accountability.

For the forgotten and entombed, few have acknowledging families remaining to mourn their passing.

People's Temple Former Headquarters:
1849 Geary Boulevard, San Francisco

IN MEMORY OF
THE VICTIMS OF
THE JONESTOWN TRAGEDY
NOV. 18, 1978
JONESTOWN, GUYANA
GUYANA EMERGENCY
RELIEF COMMITTEE

Evergreen Cemetery
6450 Camden Street, Oakland

Queen Anne Hotel: Suspicions of Scandal Amidst A Most Genteel Environment

James Fair, who the Fairmont Hotel is named after, has been classified a villain of significant proportion in late 19th century San Francisco lore. He made his fortune with the Comstock Lode through his relentless and often ruthless work ethic. He made savvy investments in real estate and railroads and parlayed this wealth into his election to the United States Senate, serving from 1881-1886.

His wealth and arrogance made him an unpopular individual with men but attractive to women. His wife might have been the exception. They married in Calaveras County in 1862 when he was a humble minor and she a boardinghouse keeper. His habitual philandering worsened as his wealth increased over the next twenty years. She divorced him mid-term in 1883 while he was based in Washington D.C.

His wife's attorney discovered during the divorce proceedings a San Francisco brothel owner and prostitute willing to testify that Fair had engaged in *criminal intercourse* and was a *habitual adulterer*. The court found the testimony credible and offered the victimized Mrs. Fair a staggering $4.25 million cash award, the couple's mansion on Pine and Jones Streets and custody of their three young children.

Fair was doubtlessly stunned by the enormity of the financial damages. He was not however overwhelmed into repentance or celibacy.

Mary Lake was the daughter of Helen and Delos Lake. She was born in Little Falls, New York. Delos moved the family to San Francisco and became one of the wealthiest local attorneys before ascending into judicial chambers. He had a family mansion built on the corner of Leavenworth and Vallejo Streets. Mary was raised in affluence becoming well educated with refined tastes.

After teaching at a few grammar schools, she opened her own academy in 1889 called the Lake Seminary, a private girl's boarding school. Her initial endeavor began modestly, but her vaulted ambitions prompted her to relocate to a recently completely 31-room Queen Anne-style mansion with dining room and impressive library. Located on the corner of Sutter and Octavia, her objective was to attract and lure enrollments from San Francisco's richest families.

Mary Lake's dream may have outstretched her financial means, but she cultivated a mentor and financial patron in James Fair. Their resulting *business* arrangement naturally aroused suspicions of scandal based on the perception they were lovers. The rumor circulated throughout California. Both denied vehemently suggestions that they had married in secret.

Lake attributed the story to an imaginative invention by unnamed enemies. Fair was guilty by reputation.

Fair insisted that he paid for the financially challenged school exclusively due to his friendship with Mary's father. Mary Lake paid $400 a month rent to Fair challenging the notion of clandestine matrimony.

When Fair died in 1894, several women came forward attempting to claim a share of his estate due to marital agreements. Actress Nettie Craven sued his estate claiming she had written proof confirming that she was his second wife. Craven was unsuccessful in her efforts and settled on marrying wealthy brewer Henry Koehler, Jr. from St. Louis.

In 1896, the school graduated their final finishing class. The *Panic of 1896* had gripped the nation financially and Lake's pockets were threadbare with Fair's permanent absence and her own depleted means. She sold the furniture, the paintings and ten pianos. The building was still owned by the Fair Estate. They leased it to the *Cosmos Club*, an elite San Francisco men's organization.

Mary Lake remained in San Francisco until 1902 before moving to Montclair, New Jersey with her half-sister. She died two years later on her 55th birthday of unknown causes. She was mourned and eulogized by the *San Francisco Call* and hundreds of former students.

Over the subsequent decades, the building declined until it was purchased, renovated and opened as the Queen Anne Hotel in the 1980s. Mary Lake's office in room #401 has frequently been cited as the source of a benevolent roaming spirit.

By all accounts Mary Lake was viewed similarly as the *San Francisco Call* eulogy.... *a keen wit and a warm, magnetic personality which endeared her to the hearts of all who had the good fortune to know her intimately.*

If her ghost indeed roams the corridors of the Queen Anne Hotel, it is certain to be a warm and gentle encounter. Hotel patrons are merely passing guests welcomed into her eternal dream finally realized.

**Queen Anne Hotel:
1590 Sutter Street, San Francisco**

Roscoe *Fatty* Arbuckle: Ten-Minute Disputed Sex Scandal

Imagine ascending to the apex of your profession as the highest paid entertainer in the world. Imagine losing it all based on being condemned for a disputed ten-minute action with no actual witnesses.

In 1921, Roscoe Fatty Arbuckle signed a three-year contract with Paramount Pictures for $1 million, an unprecedented figure at the time. Arbuckle had been a performer since his teen years traveling the West Coast on the vaudeville circuit. In 1913, at the age of 26, Arbuckle became renowned when he signed with Mack Sennett's Keystone Film Company in the role of one of the Keystone Kops. By Labor Day weekend 1921, he had arrived at his career pinnacle, set apart from his peers.

To celebrate just having finished three pictures at the same time and his new contract with Paramount, Arbuckle and a couple of friends drove up from Los Angeles to San Francisco on Saturday, September 3, 1921 for some weekend revelry. Arbuckle and friends checked into the St. Francis Hotel in San Francisco. They stayed on the twelfth floor in a suite that contained rooms 1219, 1220, and 1221 and overlooked downtown Union Square.

Over the course of a raucous three-day party at the suite, a young actress, Virginia Rappe became severely ill and died four days later. Newspapers nationally sensed a story and went ballistic. Headlines insinuated that popular silent-screen comedian Fatty Arbuckle had killed Rappe, 26-years-old with his weight while savagely raping her. It was Hollywood's first sex scandal.

To this day, no one is certain what happened exactly at that party and specifically in room #1219. Two distinct versions of events have emerged.

Maude Delmont, a renowned blackmailer became Arbuckle's principal accuser citing remarks he presumably made about Rappe before closing the door to room #1219. Partygoers heard Rappe's screams. She was found by some accounts naked and by others fully clothed and bleeding when Arbuckle opened the door. He was fully clothed. Delmont was never compelled to testify under oath with her accusations.

Arbuckle claimed that when he retired to his room to change clothes, he found Rappe vomiting in his bathroom. He then helped clean her up and led her to a nearby bed to rest. Thinking she was just overly intoxicated, he left her to rejoin the party. When he returned to the room just a few minutes later, he found Rappe on the floor. After putting her back on the bed, he left the room to get help.

Other party attendees claimed that when they entered the room, they found Rappe tearing at her clothes (something that has been claimed she did often when she was drunk). Party guests tried a number of strange treatments, including covering Rappe with ice, but her condition only worsened.

The hotel staff was contacted and Rappe was taken to another room to rest. With others looking after Rappe, Arbuckle reportedly left for a sightseeing tour and then drove back to Los Angeles.

Rappe was not taken to the hospital on that day and her condition continued to deteriorate. For three days, no one bothered to transfer her to a hospital based on their assumption that her condition was due simply to excessive drinking. Finally on Thursday, Rappe was taken to the

Wakefield Sanitarium, a maternity hospital known for giving abortions. A medical examination reportedly found no evidence of sexual assault.

Virginia Rappe died the following day from peritonitis, caused by a ruptured bladder. It was the identical death suffered by matinee idol Rudolph Valentino.

Upon her death, Arbuckle was soon arrested and charged with the murder of Virginia Rappe. Newspapers exploited the story because it sold copies. Some articles had Arbuckle crushing her with his weight and others had him raping her with a foreign object. The newspaper accounts spared no imaginative details or graphic speculations.

In the newspaper accounts, Arbuckle was presumed guilty and Virginia Rappe was an innocent 26-year-old girl. The papers excluded reporting that Rappe had a history of abortions, with some evidence indicating that she might have had another a short time before the party.

The public reaction to Arbuckle was fierce. Perhaps even more than the specific charges of rape and murder, Arbuckle became a symbol of Hollywood's immorality. Movie houses across the country immediately stopped showing Arbuckle's movies. The public was angry and used Arbuckle as a target.

Arbuckle was charged with first-degree murder, eventually reduced to manslaughter. With the scandal as front-page news on almost every newspaper, it was difficult to get an unbiased jury.

He was tried on three separate occasions, twice to hung juries. Finally he was acquitted. Public condemnation prevailed. His friends deserted him en mass. He was briefly blacklisted and his legal debts from the trials were staggering.

For the next twelve years, Arbuckle had trouble finding work. For the remainder of his career, he followed a perpetual comeback trail. The oddest of ironies was that Arbuckle signed a film contract with Warner Brothers on June 28, 1933 to act in some comedy shorts. The day after, he enjoyed a small one-year anniversary party with his new wife. Arbuckle went to bed and suffered a fatal heart attack in his sleep. He was 46.

The mystery remains whether he was the perpetrator of a violent crime or himself the victim. The only know facts during the ten decisive minutes on September 3, 1921 was that Arbuckle and Rappe ended up together in a bedroom which proved poor timing for both. Reportedly Rappe did utter the words that would damn Fatty: He did this to me.

In the end, the interpretations of these words sealed two fates; his for his immediate career demise and hers as a trivia anecdote.

Al Jolson's Untimely Demise
The St. Francis Hotel has an additional famous on site death. On October 23, 1950, actor Al Jolson (star of the 1927 first talking motion picture *The Jazz Singer*) suffered a fatal heart attack at 3 a.m. while playing gin rummy with three friends

While awaiting the doctor, he confided to his scoffing friends: *It looks like the end*. Jolson remarked that he *had no pulse*. He invited the arriving doctor to *pull up a chair and hear a story or two*. A few minutes later, he was dead.

He was en route to Hollywood to be a guest on Bing

Crosby's renowned radio show. His career was in the process of a magnificent upswing. When asked how he engineered his comeback, Jolson replied: *That was no comeback, I just couldn't get a job*.

For two decades preceding his death, he had descended from being viewed as *America's Greatest Entertainer* on the vaudeville and rag-time circuit to a theatrical has-been. A film and sequel about his life in 1946 propelled him back to the spotlight and Broadway venues. Guest appearances on prominent radio programs, entertaining troops in Korea, and marrying a lovely 21-year-old brunette elevated his professional status,

His sudden death cemented his enduring stature.

President Gerald Ford's Assassination Attempt

On September 22, 1975, just seventeen days after Charles Manson cult member Lynette *Squeaky* Fromme's attempted assassination of President Gerald Ford in Sacramento, Sara Jane Moore fired a single shot at him following a speaking engagement at the St. Francis. She used a .38 caliber revolver she had purchased earlier that morning. The gun sight was six inches off the point of impact. From forty feet away, she narrowly missed.

She wasn't allowed a second shot. Oliver Sipple, a former Marine, dived towards her and grabbed her extended arm. A second shot fired ricocheting and hitting a nearby taxi driver. He survived.

The day before the shooting, law enforcement officials had picked up Moore and confiscated her .44 caliber revolver and 113 rounds of ammunition. After being evaluated by the Secret Service, she was released based on their determination that she posed no danger to Ford.

Moore was sentenced to life in prison. In 1979, she escaped from the Alderson Federal Prison Camp in West Virginia. She was captured hours later and subsequently transferred to a federal women's prison in Dublin, California. On December 31, 2007, at age 77, Moore was released on parole. Fellow attempted assassin Fromme was released on parole in 2009. Both women are still living.

St. Francis Hotel, 335 Powell Street, San Francisco
Site of Virginia Rappe's Mysterious Illness: Suite #1219

Sentinel Building Flatiron: The Doomed Penthouse of a Political Fixer

Abe Ruef possessed the intellect and instincts of genius accompanied by serpentine ethics. He spoke eight languages, graduated from the University of California at eighteen and was admitted to the California Bar at age 21. Originally drawn to reform politics along the tenor of Theodore Roosevelt, his ambitions were eventually squandered in the quagmire of political corruption.

He was embraced by neither the Democratic nor Republican parties, so he pragmatically organized his own, the Union Labor Party. He concluded the structure and accountability of elected office too personally confining, so he schooled and sponsored candidates to dominate the San Francisco Board of Supervisors and Mayoral position. He established an intricate payoff system, which enriched him and his peers financially.

At the absolute teetering apex of his prominence in 1907, he set up his offices on the penthouse of the Sentinel Building. The building had begun construction in 1906. The skeletal framework survived the earthquake the same year. Extensive damage to the building site and surrounding downtown slowed construction significantly.

Ruef's demise arrived in the guise of a local investigation into French restaurateurs that served sexual favors for dessert to clientele on the upper floors of their establishments. All were clients of Ruef and amidst the heat of legal panic, most turned on him with damaging evidence. Sixty-five indictments were filed against Ruef for bribery of the San Francisco Supervisors. All of the Supervisors confessed before a grand jury that they had received monies from Ruef in exchange for complete immunity and not having to resign their offices.

In 1907, Ruef pleaded guilty and was convicted following a laborious and lengthy trial. The following year, he was sentenced to fourteen years in prison in San Quentin. He served five. Upon his release, he returned to his offices on the top floor. The view at the top proved lonely as his reputation and influence were shattered. He died penniless in 1936.

In 1950, the basement of the Sentinel Building was converted into an 83-seat performance venue called the *hungry i*. Entertainment began with folk singers, but in 1953, the second owner Enrico Banducci ushered in a fresh generation of stand-up comedy whose success ultimately prompted attendance lines around the block. In 1954, Banducci relocated the club to the nearby International Hotel on Jackson Street. The *hungry i* launched a legion of comic careers including Mort Sahl, Lenny Bruce, Woody Allen, Dick Gregory and even singers like Barbara Streisand.

By 1958, the Sentinel Building had significantly deteriorated and was wavering towards demolition. Rob Moor and wife purchased and renovated it renaming it the *Columbus Tower*. One and a half years later, they flipped the property selling it to the recording group, *The Kingston Trio*. During the 60s, the group used it for their corporate headquarters and installed a basement recording studio. Many music groups would use the facility and record notable albums.

In 1972, The Kingston Trio sold the building to film director Francis Ford Coppola who located his American Zoetrope film studio on site. Coppola has survived past potential financial ruin, but continues to maintain ownership. Other media related tenants occupy the commercial office space and the Café Zoetrope operates on the ground floor.

**Sentinel (Columbus Tower) Building:
916 Kearny Street, San Francisco**

Spreckels' Mansion: Encompassing Shrubbery Clouding A Legacy Laced in Secrecy

Massive hedges and shrubbery shroud and surround the Spreckels' Mansion in Pacific Heights concealing a legacy of San Francisco history that remains iconic and still visible through public monuments.

Few would remember Adolph B. Spreckels were not it for his wife Alma de Bretteville, known within society circles as *Big Alma* for her expansive personality and six foot tall height. Theirs became a legacy of ambition clouded by secrets that would ultimately restrict and shorten the life of one of them.

Adolph Spreckels was born in San Francisco in 1857 and his father Claus was the founder of the Spreckels Sugar Company. Following studies in Germany and an apprenticeship as company vice-president, he succeeded his father as president upon the 1908 death of the latter.

In 1884, he shot Michael deYoung a co-founder of the *San Francisco Chronicle* over an article intimating the sugar company had defrauded shareholders. Spreckels was acquitted of the attempted murder charge by pleading *temporary insanity*. Over the course of his life, the Spreckels and deYoung families would fuel a cultural *Hatfield vs. McCoy* relationship within San Francisco polarizing sides. The result was the California Palace of the Legion of Honor (modeled after the Parisian edition) championed by Alma Spreckels and the M. H. de Young Museum in Golden Gate Park by Michael deYoung. In a supreme twist of irony, the two institutions were merged in 1972 to become the Fine Arts Museums of San Francisco. This could have never happened while Alma or Michael was still living.

Alma de Bretteville had her own distinctive history modeling for the Dewey Monument that centers Union Square. Adolph Spreckels, a member of the selection committee, cast the tie-breaking vote from a number of entries. Although twice her age, he fell hopelessly in love with Alma and wooed her for five years until they married. She was not a naive simpleton having previously sued a former suitor, the flamboyant miner named Charlie Anderson for *personal defloweration*. With Adolph Spreckels she had a literal *sugar daddy* (which she often publicly referred him as) to finance her aspirations.

Besides the sugar company, Spreckels was president of several business concerns including railway and steamship companies. He was the San Francisco Parks Commissioner and substantially involved in the development of Golden Gate Park. *Spreckels Organ Pavilion* in San Diego's Balboa Park features the largest outdoor pipe organ in the world.

Initially the couple lived in Adolph's home in Sausalito where their first daughter was born. He soon purchased the Pacific Heights property, relocated the existing homes, and constructed a 55-room Beaux-Arts style mansion completed in 1913. The couple would have two more children together before an unpleasant secret emerged that became embarrassing public knowledge.

Spreckels had contracted syphilis before their marriage. It was reported that during their intimate years the disease had been in a latent non-contagious state. Alma claimed that she never developed the disease and her longevity probably substantiated this point. By contrast, Adolph became infirmed and wheelchair bound. He died in 1924 from pneumonia at the age of 67.

Alma's life was far from complete upon Adolph's death. She continued charity rummage sales during the Great Depression that were eventually converted into thrift shops and given to the Salvation Army. She stocked her Legion of Honor Museum and a fresh project, the Maryhill Museum of Art along the Colombia Gorge (Oregon/Washington border) with classic artwork. She owned arguably the largest collection of Auguste Rodin's sculptures in the United States.

In 1939, she married Elmer Awl, a Santa Barbara rancher and businessman. They shared a kinship for art and architectural renovation, but their collective enterprises fared poorly financially. During World War II, Awl was called away to active duty as a member of the United States Coast Guard. In his absence, Alma established several charities for the war effort. Nearing the end of the war, she discovered another embarrassing secret. Awl was having an affair with her niece. She abruptly divorced him in 1943 while he was stationed in Central America.

Her final project was the creation of the San Francisco Maritime Museum that opened in 1951. Upon her son's death in 1961, she lived primarily in seclusion visiting only her immediate family. She died like her first husband Adolph of pneumonia in 1968 at the age of 87.

Dense and concealing shrubbery has become an increasing tendency amongst Pacific Height's mansions. The desire for privacy from curious eyes creates a sense of security for property owners. The present owner of Spreckels' mansion is responsible for the current shield. Her name is Danielle Steel. As a best-selling novelist and public figure, she knows intimately the hazards and inconvenience prompted by intruding public viewing and lifestyle speculation.

Spreckels' Mansion:
2080 Washington Street, San Francisco

St. Elizabeth Center for Unwed Mothers: Mirroring Society's Change In Perception

The Daughters of Charity arrived in San Francisco on August 18, 1852. They traveled by boat, train, mule and steamer from Maryland with two Sisters dying en route from cholera. They opened an orphanage and school in a small wooden building on Market and Montgomery Streets (long disappeared).

The 25 enrolled children were fatherless and most presumably the result of abandonment or from the wombs of prostitutes. Within two years, the organization constructed a three-story brick building fronting Market Street. In 1858, the Daughters of Charity incorporated as the Roman Catholic Orphan Asylum.

In 1862, the organization purchased 57 acres on a hill in South San Francisco and opened the Mount St. Joseph Infant Asylum accommodating 300 children. The facility was serviced with door-to-door transportation by the San Francisco Trolley Company. In 1886, Mount St. Joseph opened the St. Francisco Technical trade school on Gough and Geary to instruct older girls in dressmaking, millinery, embroidery and needlework. They opened a large laundry and conducted business with hotels and private residential clients.

The Mount St. Joseph Asylum suffered minimal damage from the 1906 Earthquake, but the organization's St. Vincent School on Mission Street fared much worse. A new building was constructed on that site in 1912 and children were transferred from the Mount St. Joseph facility that shuttered three years later.

In 1921, the Daughters of Charity opened San Francisco's St. Elizabeth Infant Hospital for Unwed Mothers at 2350 Van Ness Boulevard. Within six years, the facility proved insufficient for the demand and a new building was constructed at 100 Masonic. During the succeeding fifty years, the nuns cared for women and children stigmatized by society. Their expansive trademark headwear eventually scaled down to more modest habits. Today, nuns rarely dress in uniform or habits while performing their duties and services.

Society's mores have altered significantly with regard to unwed women bearing children. Today this alternative to traditional child rearing practices is often a lifestyle preference. The St. Elizabeth Center has maintained its legal name of St. Joseph-St. Elizabeth, but identifies itself publicly as the Epiphany Center.

The child adoption process has evolved into more transparency. Children who in previous generations were born at St. Elizabeth's and put up for immediate adoption, no longer are obliged to suffer the trauma of being denied their birth parent's information.

The role of St. Elizabeth's has altered, but parental abandonment, negligence and abuse remain. The doors of the Epiphany Center stay open, necessary and funded, as their contemporary challenges and ministry are more problematical than ever.

**St. Elizabeth's Infant Hospital for Unwed Mothers:
100 Masonic, San Francisco**

Terrific Street's Momentary Flicker

A single strand of Pacific Avenue wedged into the vestiges of the former Barbary Coast district created a uniquely early 20th century pleasure zone known as *Terrific Street*. Located between Kearny and Montgomery Streets, the stretch featured dance halls, ragtime and jazz clubs, saloons and dens for prostitution.

Prior to the advent of neon, millions of blazing electric lights were visible for miles in the distance. The evening streets and sidewalks were often so congested with pedestrians, automobile access became impossible.

Some of the era's most famous performers were booked into venues including Sarah Bernhardt, Anna Pavliova, Sophie Tucker, Al Jolson and Jelly Roll Morton. The now forgotten *Texas Tommy* and *Turkey Trot* dances would be introduced on the spacious dance floors of Terrific Street. The festivities would end in 1921 following a *San Francisco Examiner's* moralistic crusade to shutter the district. The newspaper and Prohibition effectively succeeded. The Police Commission imposed severe restrictions upon the dance halls and Prohibition prevented the serving of alcohol.

Yet if masonry only had voices…

The Hippodrome, also known as the *Moulin Rouge* remains the most recognizable structure with much of the original exterior design intact. Presently operating as an art supply retailer, the building features a secret underground tunnel dating from the Barbary Coast days. Other notable establishments include *Spider Kelly's Saloon* and *Purcell's Café*,

Terrific Street cultivated a well-deserved decadent reputation. Nothing better exemplified this repute better than the *key racket* practiced by the hired girls at Spider Kelly's. After an evening of dancing with a particular regular, a male client would inquire if his dance partner would allow him to escort her home. She would reluctantly agree but only on the condition that he bought the key to her room. After paying her $5, she would hand him a key and promise to meet after closing time.

She wouldn't show and the duped patron would wander the neighborhoods vainly trying to fit their purchased keys into locked doors.

Terrific Street became reincarnated as the *International Settlement* following Prohibition between 1939-1960. Two expansive neon signs branched across the avenue acknowledging the transformation. The signs were removed around 1960.

Joining the existing clubs were the *Arabian Nights* cocktail lounge, the *Gay 'N Frisky* club, *House of Pisco*, *Monaco*, *The Barn* and *The Hurricane*. The Hurricane would evolve into the *Little Fox Theatre*, renown locally for performing Ken Kesey's *One Flew Over The Cuckoo's Nest* play during the 1970s. Milos Forman's 1975 Academy Award winning film exposed the story to millions and earned Jack Nicholson an Oscar as RP McMurphy, the lead character. Kirk Douglas had performed the identical role on Broadway and purchased the film production rights. His son Michael would ultimately successfully produce the movie despite numerous obstacles.

The historic buildings linger but the atmosphere has stilled. Broadway Street and North Beach coral the visiting and idle curious. Pacific Avenue remains dormant as a cemetery and an ideal evening parking space oasis if one doesn't mind hiking a short incline.

The Hippodrome, 555 Pacific Street, San Francisco

Purcell's Café, 520 Pacific Street, San Francisco

Spider Kelly's Saloon
574 Pacific Street (Now 570), San Francisco

Gay 'N Frisky
590 Pacific Street, San Francisco

House of Pisco
580 Pacific Street, San Francisco

Monaco
560 Pacific Street (Now 564), San Francisco

The Barn
539 Pacific Street, San Francisco

Arabian Nights
592 Pacific Street (Now 596), San Francisco

The Hurricane
533 Pacific Street, San Francisco

Whittier Mansion: A Stained Legacy Affiliated with the Nazi Reich

The Whittier Mansion in Pacific Heights was constructed in 1896 for William Frank Whittier in the Richardsonian Romanesque architectural style. The construction includes steel-reinforced brick walls and an imposing facing of Arizona red sandstone.

Whittier was the head of what would later become Pacific Gas and Electric Company (PG & E). His family occupied the 30-room mansion until 1938 surviving the 1906 Earthquake and his death in 1917.

Economic duress prompted his daughter to sell the building in 1938. Adolph Hitler's Third Reich was an enthusiastic buyer with the early stages of World War II raging in Europe. The mansion became San Francisco's German Consulate. Consul General Fritz Wiesemann, his wife and children resided on the top floor. The first floor Consular offices were set up with desks and safes, barred doors and piled file cabinets in the former dining room. The consular staff was stationed in a suite of rooms on the second floor.

Wiesemann, his family and staff were ordered to leave the United States in mid July 1941, but complications arose regarding his boarding a Japanese steamer as he awaited a guarantee of safe passage from the British government. The group instead boarded a plane from San Francisco routing him to New York and finally Portugal. The consular party eventually reached Germany via a sailing vessel.

Wiesemann had an unusual and intimate relationship with Hitler starting in World War I where as a captain, he was Hitler's superior officer. In 1933 when Hitler rose to the chancellorship of Germany, he summoned Wiesemann to

Berlin. The former captain had been living on his Bavarian farm located at the base of the Alps in retirement.

Upon his arrival, he became a close confidant of Hitler and was described in a *San Francisco Chronicle* article dated December 11, 1937 as *a top personal aid in the chancellery household, a super private secretary handing the most confidential matters.* It was suggested that Wiesemann *probably knows more about Adolf Hitler than any man living.*

Following the bombing of Pearl Harbor on December 7, 1941 and the subsequent declarations of war against Japan and Germany, the Whittier Mansion and its remaining contents were seized. Upon Wiesemann's return to Germany, he never regained his prior status or level of confidence with Hitler.

During the war years, the building was bolted shut. The property was subsequently auctioned off in 1950 and resold twice later before being occupied by the California Historical Society from 1956 to 1991.

The house is rumored to be haunted, but not by its former Nazi occupiers. The culprit is rumored to be the pleasure-seeking son Billy of original owner William Whittier. Billy lived off his father's money, was notoriously idle and developed an acute fondness for wine and women. He apparently never wished to leave the premises even with the changes in ownership.

So he never has.

William Frank Whittier Mansion:
2090 Jackson, San Francisco

William Westerfeld House: The Ultimate 1960s Crash Pad

In the 1870s, German-born confectioner William Westerfeld arrived in San Francisco and established a chain of successful bakeries. In 1889, he hired builder Henry Geilfuss to design and construct a 28-room mansion with adjoining rose garden and carriage house. When he died in 1895, the home was sold to John Mahony whose company rebuilt the St. Francis Hotel and Palace Hotel following the 1906 Earthquake. In the aftermath, Mahony replaced the rose garden with apartments to address the city's dire need for accommodations.

The house became a pivotal cornerstone in San Francisco's twentieth century cultural evolution. In 1928, a collective of Czarist Russians purchased the house and converted the ground level ballroom into a nightclub called *Dark Eyes*. Upper floors were employed for meeting rooms by the formerly influential exiles prompting the building's informal moniker the *Russian Embassy*.

In 1948, the mansion was converted into a 14-unit apartment that accommodated African-American jazz musicians playing in the nearby Fillmore district for the next two decades.

During the 1960s, the building hosted a fifty-member collective called the *Calliope Company*. Underground filmmaker Kenneth Anger, while in residence, filmed *Invocation of My Demon Brother* starring a cast of infamy including Manson family member Bobby Beausoleil, Church of Satan founder Anton LaVey with a soundtrack by Mick Jagger. LaVey conducted many satanic rituals in the ballroom as well as the top floor tower. Being a nearly daily visitor, he had a large pentagram etched into the

165

floorboards. Author Tom Wolfe noted the property in his book *The Electric Kool-Aid Acid Test*.

Throughout the decade, the location was a familiar crash pad for the Grateful Dead, Janis Joplin and the Big Brother and the Holding Company. Members of the Family Dog occupied the premises and promoted rock concerts at the Polk Gulch based Avalon Ballroom between 1966 to 1969, the peak of the counterculture movement.

Sex, drugs and rock n' roll was replaced by a massive Western Addition urban renewal project that felled 6,000 Victorian-era structures over a 60-block area. The Westerfeld was spared this *architectural heritage horror* campaign. New owner Jim Siegel began a significant overall renovation in 1986 and the results remain timeless.

When surveying the phantom imprint of lost landmarks and their sterile *modern* replacements, one may only shrug and imagine what influences the city planners were then inhaling.

William Westerfeld House:
1198 Fulton, San Francisco

The Zebra Killings: A Racially Intended Genocide?

After over forty years following their commission, certain murders haunt and still scald. Their secrets and searing hot implications remain immune to in-depth public and media excavation. Feature films will not be financed. Memorials and reenactments for public remembrance are nonexistent. The killings are simply too lethal to the touch and remain barely superficially reported and archived. A desire to forget this story has buried it for over four decades. But did the murder spree ever truly conclude?

The most disturbing series of San Francisco homicides in the 1970s were unquestionably the Zebra murders. Two principle reasons still provoke outrage over the serial killings amongst those who choose to remember. The killings were exclusively racially motivated and a cover-up by law enforcement agencies masked the territorial extent and number of actual killings.

Between August 1973 and April 1974 within San Francisco alone, fifteen execution-style murders and eight serious assaults leaving survivors were publicly documented. Amongst the surviving victims was future San Francisco Mayor Art Agnos, then a member of the California Commission on Aging. Agnos was attending a community meeting on Potrero Hill and shot twice in the back. He miraculously survived the shooting.

Police identified the case as Zebra after the special police radio Z band they had assigned for the investigation. The designation seemed equally appropriate given the racially motivated nature of the attacks. Twenty-two individual crimes within a six-month spree were attributed exclusively to at least four convicted African-American suspects. Evidence suggests however, that their capture and conviction was merely the extreme tip of a much larger targeted genocide.

The term *racial genocide* conjures up comparatives with recent and twentieth century holocausts and mass exterminations. The intent behind the acts seemed no different and ultimately become a question of comparison and semantics. At what victim quantifying level do admittedly racially motivated killings qualify as genocide?

During the 179 days of terror, the murders caused widespread panic in San Francisco. People gathered in groups as a safety precaution or simply remained indoors. The city suffered economically as tourists stayed away. In reaction, a significantly increased police presence was ordered throughout the city.

The killings continued. Police remained baffled by an apparent lack of motive, the brutality, and hatred exhibited by the perpetrators.

Certain consistencies were known about the killings. All of the shootings involved two different .32 caliber pistols. The murders were excessively swift, brutal, and savagely executed. All of the victims were Caucasian and most either elderly, slightly built or defenseless. All of the killers were identified as African-Americans. Most of the victims were shot multiply and generally to the body (enabling unintentional survival for some). One victim was raped and two were hacked to death by machetes and knives.

A special task force was formed to try to solve and stop the murders. On the evening of December 28, 1973, five shootings alone were recorded with four fatalities.

After the final killing, out of desperation and a lack of

concrete leads, local law enforcement authorities initiated a program of controversial racial profiling that today would be inconceivable. African-American males resembling the composite sketches of two suspected killers were systematically stopped, searched and questioned. Once they'd completed an examination process, they were given a specially imprinted Zebra interrogation card, which they could display to police officers if stopped again.

This action by the police provoked vocal and widespread criticism from the African-American community. A US District Judge within a week ruled the program unconstitutional and the operation was suspended. Although the program did not result in any arrests, it was suggested that it prompted an informer within the murder ring who resembled one of the drawings to come forward. Aside from his fear of capture, a $30,000 reward he claimed ultimately pierced the veil of secrecy behind the killings.

Anthony Harris, an estranged employee from the Black Self-Help Moving and Storage on Market Street met with Zebra case detectives in Oakland. He provided an avalanche of incriminating evidence and to solidify his credibility, detailed precise facts about a homicide that had not been reported by local news sources.

Harris was present at many of the killings but denied actually killing anyone.

Harris provided the police with names, dates, addresses and details. His information provided enough information to issue arrest warrants against multiple suspects. Harris subsequently sought, and received, immunity for his help in breaking the Zebra case. He, his girlfriend and her child were relocated and given new identities. Under extreme pressure to end the bloodshed and apprehend the responsible perpetrators, many observers questioned whether police granted immunity to an individual equally responsible. Harris narrowly escaped his own execution before testifying by organizers of the massacres.

On May 1, 1974 simultaneous raids during the pre-dawn hours were made, resulting in the arrests of Larry Craig Green and J.C.X. Simon in an apartment building on Grove Street. More suspects were arrested fearing their flight at the Black Self-Help Moving and Storage's facility. Of the seven arrested that day, four were released for lack of conclusive evidence including the manager and his assistant at the moving facility. Manuel Moore was the only additional detainee along with Green and Simon.

What surfaced publicly following the arrests was the existence of a sordid murder cult, called the *Death Angels,* aimed exclusively towards the extermination of the Caucasian race. The Nation of Islam Mosque #26 based in San Francisco, then located at the Fillmore Auditorium (or a splinter sect within) was prominently fingered as the conspiratorial organization behind the attacks. Charges against the organization were never pursued in court.

The Nation of Islam group, headquartered in Chicago, paid the attorney fees for Green, Simon and Moore. They did not pay purposely for Jessie Lee Cooks as he had earlier pled guilty for a spree-related murder and was incarcerated. Pleading guilty for any crime was considered an affront to the group's separatist philosophy. He was charged simultaneously along with the other three members for his participation in the murder spree.

The trial of the accused started on March 3, 1975. Exhaustive efforts were employed by defense attorneys to discredit Harris. Their tactics proved to no avail as he methodically and exhaustively spilled all of the grisly details over 12 days of testimony.

One of the two .32 caliber Beretta automatic pistols used in many of the later killings had been recovered and traced methodically and directly to the manager and his assistant of the Black Self-Help Moving and Storage facility. The two were never indicted.

The trial featured the testimony of 108 witnesses, 8,000 pages totaling 3.5 million words worth of transcripts, and culminating in what was then the longest criminal trial in California history. Larry Green, J. C. X. Simon, Manuel Moore and Jessie Lee Cooks were convicted of first-degree murder and conspiracy to commit first-degree murder in 1976. Despite the length of the trial and mountainous testimony and evidence, the jury unanimously arrived at their verdict within 18 hours of deliberation.

Larry Green is currently serving his sentence at the California State Prison in Vacaville and Jessie Lee Cooks at RJ Donovan Correctional Facility in San Diego. J. C. X. Simon expired in his prison cell near midnight on March 12, 2015 in San Quentin and Manuel Moore died on November 15, 2017 at the California Health Care Facility in Stockton. There is no public record of personal remorse expressed by either killer towards any of his victims.

The most troubling element of the Zebra serial killings was the extent and geographical magnitude of the murderous spree. There was significant evidence introduced to indicate the San Francisco killings were only a smaller component of a more aggressive statewide and potentially national program of extermination. None of the responsible organizers of the mass killing program were apprehended, publicly identified or punished.

In 1979, writer Clark Howard's book *Zebra* was published. Howard's work has been acknowledged by numerous credible sources as the most definitive, thorough and authoritative book on the murders. Using court records, police reports, witnesses and interviews with the killers themselves, Howard was able to piece together the horrid details behind the murders and the unrelenting hatred that inspired the killers.

Howard's book detailed the sobering criteria employed by the responsible cell group within the Nation of Islam that were designed solely towards the objective of murder. Howard described the vicious, sometimes impulsive and universally cowardly nature of the attacks.

According to his book, the minimum criteria for becoming a Death Angel required the confirmed killing of 9 white males, 5 white women and 4 white children. The book cited that by October 20, 1973, at least 15 accredited death assassins were operating within California. Based on their requirement criteria, this would result in a minimum of 270 fatalities.

Other published sources have speculated that as many as 50 qualified operatives were at work within the state. Their blood counts were employed as recruiting devices by massacre organizers to swell the prospective killing base of fresh inductees.

The book introduced chilling confirmation that the California attorney general's office had compiled a list of 71 execution-style murders committed around the state. The murders were facilitated with either a machete or pistol, in which, the killer or killers was always a well dressed and groomed youngish black man, and the victim always white.

In addition to San Francisco, the murders were carried out in Oakland, San Jose, Emeryville, Berkeley, Long Beach, Signal Hill, Santa Barbara, Palo Alto, Pacifica, San Diego, Los Angeles, and in the counties of San Mateo, Santa Clara, Los Angeles, Contra Costa, Ventura and Alameda. This intended racial genocide program was estimated by some sources to have begun approximately three years before the San Francisco killings.

Regardless of the exact toll, the heartlessness behind synchronized murder becomes sickening reading. What sort of monster(s) or organization could condone such depravity? It remains unimaginable to assume that only four individuals should bear the sole responsibility for such heinous behavior. Yet only four insignificant foot soldiers ultimately did.

None of the remaining two convicts have ever publicly asked forgiveness or expressed shame for their actions despite forty years of incarceration. Were compassion and humanity possible emotions to accompany their blind obedience? Do they share any resentment towards bearing the punishment for the acts alone?

Their superiors eluded public disclosure, capture and accountability.

The most widely circulating rationalization then by authorities for downplaying the fatalities was to avoid widespread public panic and alarm. In truth, this underexposure potentially created more victims unknowingly vulnerable.

The fatalities in the San Francisco spree included Quita Hague, Frances Rose, Saleem Erakat, Paul Dancik, Marietta DiGirolamo, Ilario Bertuccio, Neal Moynihan, Mildred Hosler, Tana Smith, Vincent Wollin, John Bambic, Jane Holly, Thomas Rainwater, Nelson Shields IV and one anonymous victim labeled John Doe #169.

The seriously wounded included Richard Hague, Ellen Linder, Art Agnos, Angela Roselli, Roxanne McMillian, Linda Story, Ward Anderson and Terry White.

It has been over four decades since the Zebra Killings. With the exception of Clark Howard's book, little has been written since that has profoundly re-evaluated the murders. San Francisco civic victim memorial ceremonies or remembrances have never been held. The 23 victims remain essentially published footnotes and forgotten. The primary buildings involved in the drama have been remodeled, renumbered and facades freshened. Layers of applied paint can never completely cover the stainage.

Not everyone has conveniently forgotten the terror and carnage.

A trail of human extermination leaves many witnesses and survivors within its wake. Their eyewitness stories have the capacity to preserve the indignity for generations. This criminal narrative may have temporarily disappeared from the mainstream media and public consciousness but for many it will never remained buried.

The callousness and evil behind the attacks remain a permanent scandal. The violence symbolized an unjustified affront against both humanity and public disclosure. For the present time, there appears little interest to penetrate deeper.

175

**Black Self-Help Moving Building:
1630-1645 Market Street, San Francisco**

Two Killer's Residence:
844 Grove Street (renumbered 870), San Francisco

The Hagues: 24th and Minnesota Streets, San Francisco

178

Frances Rose: 100 Block of Laguna Street, San Francisco

Saleem Hassan Erakat: 452 Larkin Street, San Francisco

Paul Dancik:
Corner Haight and Buchanan Streets, San Francisco

Mariena DiGirolamo:
Corner of Haight Street and Divisadero, San Francisco

Ilario Bertuccio:
Bancroft and Phelps, San Francisco

Angela Roselli: Near Grove and Central, San Francisco

Neal Moynihan:
Civic Center Hotel, 20 12th Street, San Francisco

Mildred Hosler: Block of Gough Street Below Market Street, San Francisco

Tana Smith:
Geary and Divisadero Streets, San Francisco

Vincent Wollin:
709 Scott Street, San Francisco

Jane Holly:
1440 Silver Avenue, San Francisco

Roxanne McMillian:
102 Edinburgh, San Francisco

Thomas Rainwater:
Bertie Manor Lane at Geary Street, San Francisco

Ward Anderson and Terry White:
Corner Hayes and Steiner Street, San Francisco

EAST BAY AREA

David Nadel: The Death of a Man and Rebirth of a Performance Icon

The Ashkenaz Club is Berkeley's most renowned live world music club venue. Many of the organization's supporters claim Ashkenaz was multicultural before the term was even coined.

Performance artist David Nadel founded Ashkenaz in 1973 after relocating from Los Angeles to attend UC Berkeley. Nadel began the center as a collective with a dance troupe and expanded into the present location on San Pablo Avenue. The organization drew its name from his Ashkenazi Jewish ancestry and resembles an Eastern European synagogue.

On December 19, 1996, an unruly patron, Juan Rivera Perez was ejected from the club. He returned a half hour later knocking on the front door. Nadel answered and was greeted by a handgun shot to his head. He died two days later.

Perez was reportedly enrolled in an *English As A Second Language* program and was attending the nightclub as part of a graduation program. He reportedly fled to his native Mexico, which historically has been uncooperative in extraditing violent criminals back to the United States.

He remains at large today.

In the wake of Nadel's murder, a group of Ashkenaz patrons purchased the building and re-opened the club six months later. It continues to operate today.

Nadel was renowned as a global activist and supporter of numerous and varied causes. One might dispute his political leanings, but no one challenged his generosity and passion. Nadel's death widened the base of ownership participation but sadly his killer will probably never face accountability for his murder.

Ashkenaz Club Killing:
1317 San Pablo Avenue, Berkeley

Chauncey Bailey: The Price of Constitutional Protection

Our Freedom of the Press is a constitutional protection that Chauncey Bailey paid dearly for to defend. It is ironic that amidst today's spin journalism and advertising sponsored content, reporting the truth remains as potent and relevant as ever.

Chauncey Bailey, Jr. was an American journalist, noted for his writings primarily on African-American issues. His most prominent position was as editor of The Oakland Post from June 2007 until his death less than two months later.

At 7:30 a.m. on August 2, 2007, Bailey was shot dead execution-style on a downtown Oakland street as he followed his customary route from his apartment to work. His lone assassin fled on foot to a parked van and drove off. Bailey was killed while working on an exposé about the finances, contract killings and fraud involved with *Your Black Muslim Bakery* and the organization's impending bankruptcy. The story had been temporarily withheld from publication due to its potentially incendiary nature.

The sidewalk stretch of 14th Street where Bailey was slain is less than 50 feet from intersecting Alice Street, where the getaway vehicle was parked. A mature tree to the right and a fenced-in postal distribution facility to the left with scattered landscaped shrubbery shade the concrete. Numerous pedestrians pass the location daily en route to their workplaces or simply to loiter in the neighborhood.

The killing site was unremarkable and could be transplanted to any major urban center. The brazenness and early hour of the killing were the most shocking elements. Shootings in downtown Oakland streets ceased to become novelty years ago. The confrontation between killer and victim was brief. Bailey very likely knew his fate, his killer and the motive.

The notoriety of Bailey's killing immediately collapsed the fortunes of *Your Black Muslim Bakery*.

Early the following morning, Oakland Police officers and SWAT team members closed off a number of blocks of San Pablo Avenue. Their search warrants and area of focus included homes and business properties of the bakery facility, which operated two business sites within the area.

The bakery and its operators were a Black Muslim splinter organization originally founded by Yusuf Bey, and consequently led by his son Yusuf Bey IV. The pre-dawn raids followed a two-month investigation into a variety of violent crimes, including kidnapping and murder. Bailey's death prompted immediate response and caught the residents unprepared.

During the raid, police arrested Devaughndre Broussard, who confessed to both stalking and then killing Bailey on orders from Yusuf Bey IV. Bailey's murder weapon was recovered during the raid. Bey IV denied ordering the killings. It wasn't until April 2009 once Broussard agreed to cooperate with prosecutors that he and one of his bakery associate's Antoine Mackey were charged in Bailey's killing.

On the same day after Bailey's death, U.S. Bankruptcy Judge Edward Jellen ordered the immediate financial liquidation of the bakery. The organization's fragile facade collapsed swiftly and definitively.

Bey IV and Mackey were found guilty in June 2011 of

three counts of murder in ordering the deaths of Bailey and two other former bakery associates. Bey IV is presently interned at the California Medical Facility in Vacaville following a term at the Salinas Valley State Prison. Mackey was convicted of murdering one bakery associate and helping Broussard kill Bailey. He is serving his sentence now at the Salinas Valley State Prison following a stay at the California State Prison facility in Lancaster. Both first-degree murder charges carry a mandatory sentence of life in prison without the possibility of parole.

Devaughndre Broussard, the triggerman, accepted a plea deal in exchange for his testimony and was sentenced to 25 years in prison. He originally served his term at the Salinas Valley State Prison before being transferred to the LaPalma Correctional Center in Eloy, Arizona. He has since been transferred to the Sierra Conservation Center in Jamestown, California.

Chauncey Bailey was the first journalist killed over a domestic story in the United States since 1976. That year, Don Bolles of *The Arizona Republic* died in a car bombing. Bailey's death is a reminder despite the flaws of modern journalism, its role remains critical to preserving a free society.

Chauncey Bailey Jr. Killing Site:

Approaching the corner of Alice and 14th Street, Oakland

The Helzer Brothers: Children of Thunder

A lethal cocktail mix of drug use, schizophrenia and religious fanaticism manifested into a series of monstrous killings by the Helzer Brothers.

Justin Helzer and Glenn Helzer, (who went by his middle name Taylor), murdered five people as part of a bizarre blackmail scheme. Taylor Helzer was a stockbroker and self-prophesied prophet. An important element of his doctrine included raising money for a religious movement oriented towards bringing Jesus Christ's return to Earth. As the figurehead of his organization of three, he orchestrated a sequence of killings driven by inner voices and spirits.

Following high school graduation, the Helzer boys fulfilled a two-year Mormon missionary requirement of service. Taylor's mission was in Brazil and Justin's in Texas. Upon their return to northern California, Justin became a cable installer and Taylor a stockbroker in downtown San Francisco.

Taylor followed a traditional suburban lifestyle upon his return, marrying and fathering two daughters. The façade endured three years before he wearied of the restraints of being a proper husband and Mormon. He rebelled against the strict religious living code and began liberally indulging in drugs and sexual relations outside of marriage. During this stage of mutiny, he began wearing exclusively black clothing and neglecting his personal hygiene.

The Mormon Church reportedly excommunicated him for his profane behavior.

His erratic behavior and drug use intensified during 2000. He initiated a delusional campaign to take over the

Mormon Church involving a variety of criminal schemes to facilitate his designs. He founded a self-help group called Impact America and recruited his impressionable younger brother Justin and an acquaintance Dawn Godman as participants. Godman moved into their rental house in Concord.

From the outlet, fraud and killing in God's name were accepted cornerstones agreed upon by the trio in their strategic planning.

Among the money raising ploys debated included recruiting underage Brazilian girls as prostitutes for wealthy businessmen that could evolve into blackmail revenue. Another tactic considered was to adopt Brazilian orphans who would be trained to assassinate the top Mormon leadership in Utah. The subsequent void would pave the entrance for Taylor to assume leadership of the institution.

In 2000, the conspirators officially called themselves *The Children of Thunder*. To fuel their ambitious agenda, Taylor ultimately resorted to more common means of fundraising. He decided to extort some of his elderly former clients with the goal of obtaining in excess of $100,000 seed money.

Taylor at the same time began dating 22-year-old Selina Bishop, the daughter of musician Elvin Bishop. Her designed role in his plot was to open a checking account enabling him to launder money he intended to extort from his former clients. This account Taylor reasoned would remove his name from all illicit activities exposing only Bishop. She was infatuated by him and completely unaware of the implications involved by opening the account (at least initially). She later became expendable.

The initial target of his extortion plot was a former client (from a list of five) who lived in Walnut Creek but was not home during their visit on Sunday, July 30. Their second choice, Ivan Stineman, 85, and his wife, Annette, 78, completely trusted Taylor having been acquainted as both clients and friends over the years. Reportedly, the same or the following day, both Helzer brothers, wearing suits and carrying briefcases, knocked on their door and escorted them over to the their Concord residence.

During the ensuing hours, Annette Stineman reportedly phoned the manager of the Concord branch of her stock brokerage nervously indicating she wished to liquidate her investments. Although the request was unusual, the manager honored it.

Prosecutors speculated that the trio then forced the Stinemans to drink Rohypnol, a sedative and known date rape drug, and made them write out two checks, one for $33,000, and the other for $67,000 to Selina Bishop. Taylor thought the retirees would overdose on the Rohypnol and die, but they didn't. Instead the brothers in front of a horrified Godman savagely killed them. The following day Godman deposited the checks into Bishop's account.

On August 3rd, the murderous siblings accompanied by Godman, killed Selina Bishop in their home to silence her after she collected the money from the account on their behalf unaware about the homicidal plot. The bodies of Selina Bishop and the Stinemans were dismembered and stuffed into nine black duffel bags, which were later fished out by divers from the Sacramento-San Joaquin River Delta.

During the pre-dawn hours of August 4, Taylor shot dead Bishop's mother, 45-year-old Jennifer Villarin, and her boyfriend, James Gamble, 54, for fear that they would go to police once her daughter was reported missing. Jennifer Villarin had once met Taylor Helzer and knew that he had been dating her daughter. Helzer had a spare key to her daughter's studio apartment where her mother was housesitting and had entered undetected.

The brother's attempts to hide the crimes unraveled quickly. On Monday, August 7th, sheriff's deputies drove to the Helzer's rental house with a search warrant. They wanted to look for the gun that was used to kill Villarin and Gamble. All of the tenants were home when they knocked on the door. When the deputies swept through the house, they found ecstasy, hallucinogenic mushrooms, and drug paraphernalia, but no gun, according to the police report. The cops arrested the trio on drug possession charges.

Later that day, the first two duffel bags, one containing a human head, the other a torso, floated to the surface of the Mokelumne River. After the rest of the bags were recovered, experts at the Contra Costa County Crime Lab used DNA analysis to identify the victims, which confirmed preliminary findings made using dental records.

Authorities charged all three roommates with 18 felonies, including murder, extortion, and kidnapping. It would require four more years for juries to sort through the tangled details of the case and sentence the last of the trio for crimes they'd committed.

Faced with solid evidence against all three, Godman struck a deal with prosecutors. In exchange for pleading guilty to five counts of murder and testifying against the Helzer brothers, she avoided the death penalty and got a sentence of 38 years to life in prison. She is currently incarcerated at the Central California Women's Facility in Chowchilla.

In March 2004, Taylor Helzer entered a surprise guilty plea, and his attorney relayed Taylor's impromptu confession to a stunned courtroom. On June 16, a jury convicted Justin Helzer of 11 counts, including murder, extortion and kidnapping for his role in the killings. He pleaded not guilty by reason of insanity.

On April 16, 2013, Justin Helzer, 41, was found dead in his single cell at San Quentin Prison. Helzer used a sheet tied to his cell bars to hang himself. An earlier suicide attempt two years earlier had left the death row inmate blind when he stabbing himself repeatedly in the eye with pens and pencils. Glenn Taylor Helzer remains on death row at San Quentin, a dishonored prophet in exile.

Children of Thunder Base:
5370 Saddlewood Court, Concord

Port Chicago Mutiny and the Inconvenience of Protesting Authority

In times of War, principles of defiance and conscience are often casually dismissed or punished due to the implication that orders from an established chain of command are infallible.

At the Concord Naval Weapons Station at Port Chicago located on Suisun Bay, predominantly African-American sailors and civilians were ordered to hand load live munitions into cargo vessels bound for the Pacific Theatre during World War II. Safety training was lax, speed and haste necessitated and the explosive cargoes highly volatile.

A sequence of human and mechanical errors led to the inevitable worst-case nightmare during the loading process of the Liberty ship SS E. A. Bryan on July 17, 1944. The ship contained 5,292 barrels of heavy fuel oil and 4,600 tons of explosives (40% of capacity) following four days of nonstop loading. At approximately 10:00 p.m., the munitions detonated stimulating an unimaginable inferno and damage.

Three hundred and twenty men were killed and another three hundred ninety were reported injured. Owing to the urgency of the war effort, operations at the base resumed almost right afterwards. The conditions remained unsafe and primed to repeat.

One month later, hundreds of African-American servicemen refused to load munitions. Their defiance became known as the *Port Chicago Mutiny*. Fifty of their peers were convicted of mutiny and sentenced to 15 years in prison and hard labor. They were labeled the *Port Chicago 50*. Each was dishonorably discharged. Forty-seven were released in January 1946 and the remaining three served additional months in prison.

During their original trial, questions were raised regarding the legality of the court-martial and the racial implications that targeted African-American soldiers exclusively in this hazardous work. The Navy reconvened the court-martial board in 1945, but merely affirmed the guilt of the convicted men. This ruling added insult to an already grievous injury.

Repercussions would follow. In February 1946 following the release of the imprisoned sailors, the Navy began a process of examining their segregation process. While not admitting error, the Naval forces began a desegregation process. In 1994, a national memorial was dedicated to the lives lost in the disaster.

It wasn't until 2019 that a congressional resolution both recognized the victims of the explosion and officially exonerated the fifty men court-martialed. For the *Port Chicago 50* this empty acknowledgement arrived far too late to repair their permanently decimated reputations and later civilian lives. The majority are now deceased. At the same time more than 2,200 acres of former eastern Station land was turned over to the East Bay Regional Park District which plans to make this land the center of a new park.

Perhaps in certain circles their disobedience was dismissed as simple cowardice, subversion or as victims, collateral damage from war. Authority attempts to silence and subjugate outrage and protest even amidst the worst of national policy decisions. World War II was certainly justified, but the Navy's arrogance towards these men unconscionable. Legitimately practiced democracy and freedom of speech can be inconvenient distractions.

The inland portion of the Concord Naval Weapons Station was closed in 2005. For a short time longer, entry remains restricted prohibiting outside public visitation. Plans for the acquired grounds include housing, businesses, a college campus and other developments.

Historically protests and anti-war protesters have lined the perimeter fencing. On September 1, 1987 Vietnam veteran Brian Wilson, beginning a hunger strike, positioning himself on the railroad tracks protesting illegal arms shipments to Nicaragua.

A munitions train powered through at 17 miles an hour, three times the legal speed limit. The 200, 000 pound locomotive severed his legs and left him with multiple broken bones and a plate in his head. Authorities immediately labeled him a *domestic terrorist*. The conductor was never punished nor ever revealed if he regretted his actions.

Americans universally lauded the *Tank Man*, an unknown protestor who defied the Chinese military by standing defiantly in front of a tank column leaving Tiananmen Square on June 5, 1989. His alleged name was Wang Weilin and he was rumored to have been killed shortly afterwards. The Chinese government has never acknowledged the incident. An iconic video and photo is evidence that the event actually occurred.

It seems lost on many that protest is one of guarantees of constitutional freedom. If we can admire an unknown foreign citizen for staging an irrational act of defiance, why can't we honor our own citizenry that simply chooses to disagree, particularly when they are later proven correct?

**Concord Naval Weapons Station:
5110 Port Chicago Highway, Concord**

Dr. Marcus Foster: The Marginalized Assassination

Perhaps the most tragic and least remembered link from the notorious Patty Hearst abduction was the November 6, 1973 assassination of Dr. Marcus Foster, the Oakland School District Superintendent. His needless death launched the public ascension of the Symbionese Liberation Army (SLA) into a revolutionary terrorist organization. Three gunmen, Joseph Remiro, Russell Little and probably SLA leader Donald DeFreeze ambushed Foster and his deputy superintendent Robert Blackburn near their parked cars at dusk following a school board meeting.

The parking lot today remains paved and lined as it did during the 1973 slaying. The Oakland Unified School district building has fallen into decay and disrepair. The building and parking lot are fenced in and the only evidence of activity is the sole security guard employed daily to prevent vandalism and break-ins.

Foster was killed instantly sustaining between seven to nine cyanide tipped bullets. Blackburn was critically wounded but miraculously survived. A team of surgeons labored throughout the night to stop the bleeding and prevent further internal organ damage from twenty-three entry and exit shotgun wounds and multiple heart stoppages.

Ironically upon Blackburn's recovery, he assumed Foster's Superintendent position for the next two years. Professionally he continued a distinguished academic career until his death on September 10, 2016.

What Foster may have accomplished as Oakland's Superintendent and beyond is impossible to gauge. He was universally respected after arriving from Philadelphia in

1970 to assume the head position.

His death was both senseless and erroneously motivated. The SLA assassins targeted Foster because they believed he supported student ID cards and a police presence in schools. In reality, Foster had opposed the identification cards and publicly announced that he would not allow police officers in the schools.

The deterioration of the Oakland Unified School District, encompassing over 120 schools, has been well documented. The carcass symbolized by the former administration building is testament to decades of administrative incompetence, urban decay and financial mismanagement. The district declared bankruptcy in 2011.

Two of the assassins, Joseph Remiro and Russell Little, were arrested after a shootout with police in Concord in January 1974 and charged with Foster's murder. The kidnapping of Patty Hearst on February 4th was an idiotic attempt by the SLA to bargain their release and divert attention away from the Foster fiasco.

The SLA was uninformed and naïve about their potential negotiating adversary. Then California governor Ronald Reagan would have never sanctioned a prisoner exchange in any form.

On May 17, 1974, the third suspect Donald DeFreeze was involved in a shoot-out with the Los Angeles Police force. Outgunned and trapped with five other SLA members, DeFreeze committed suicide by shooting himself in the right side of his head while apparently burning alive.

Convicted in 1974 for Foster's murder, Joseph Remiro began serving a life sentence at the Pelican Bay State

Prison. He remains incarcerated today at San Quentin following an extended stay at the California State Prison facility in Lancaster. Russell Little was also convicted of first-degree murder but due to a technical error in the jury instructions, was later retried and acquitted. He was released in 1983 and reportedly changed both his name and his residence to Hawaii.

The SLA never regrouped or captured the same level of media attention following the fatal Los Angeles shoot-out. Other members disbanded or were imprisoned over the subsequent years. Their impact on society ultimately proved as empty as their political agenda and rhetoric.

Dr. Marcus Foster Slaying:
Rear parking lot of former Oakland Unified School
District, 1025 Second Avenue, Oakland

Fat Lady Bar and Restaurant: Painting or Madame?

The building was constructed in 1884 as a bar and restaurant called the *Overland House*. Author Jack London lived nearby and likely frequented the establishment. Reliable sources confirm that the *Overland* was a notable house of ill-repute.

How did the *fat lady* moniker intervene? Was she the *Overland's* Madame as fanciful imaginations might suggest? An account on the current restaurant's website suggests this theory accompanied by a second story involving a large-scale rotund nude painted by an Oakland superior court judge's son. The distinctive painting needed a hanging location. The Overland's proprietors felt it enhanced their standing with a particular legal authority. Thus perhaps a marriage of convenience was conceived.

The current Fat Lady Bar and Restaurant opened in May 1970 and is decorated throughout with Victorian décor, beveled glass doors, Tiffany lamps, Brentwood chairs, stained and leaded glass signs and a back bar that was shipped around the horn at the turn of the twentieth century.

The mystery behind the name merits a glass of claret for reflection...or perhaps a bottle for a fuller examination.

Fat Lady Bar and Restaurant:
201 Washington Street, Oakland

Ghost Ship Warehouse Fire: Captained Without a Rudder or Clue

Depending upon your perspective, the Ghost Ship warehouse in Oakland was either an experimental artist collective or a poorly managed commercial rental and event staging scam. Both options became pertinent when on the late evening of December 2, 2016, a fire erupted incinerating the interior of the warehouse and killing 36 people trapped within. That evening the facility was hosting a concert that had attracted approximately fifty spectators.

The warehouse was originally constructed in 1930 and was once part of a milk bottling plant. Later it was used for the storage of metal pipes. In 1988, Chor Ng who reportedly owns seventeen properties in the Bay Area purchased it. Ng leased the warehouse in 2013 to Derick Almena.

Almena and his assistant Max Harris loosely operated the facility, benefiting from a chronically tight Oakland rental market and sloppy enforcement of building codes. In the chaos following the destructive fire, published reports circulated regarding a litany of complaints lodged against the facility concerning hazardous garbage and construction debris, blight, and illegal interior construction.

The most telling response to these complaints involved a visitation to the warehouse by city inspectors three weeks before the fire. The inspectors knocked on the front door. When no one answered, they simply left. There is no record of a return visit. The City of Oakland's planning director revealed that the building had not been inspected for three decades.

A cursory glance of the warehouse's exterior makes it

abundantly clear the facility was never intended or designed to be residential quarters or a performance venue. Permits and licensing were never issued for either and would have been denied if anyone had bothered to pursue the application process. Given that other larger attended events including late night rave parties were frequent occurrences, regard for proper standards and safety was never a priority.

The question of accountability surfaced immediately as the ashes cooled.

On the evening of the fatal performance, Max Harris served as the doorman, while Almena and his family were securely lodged in an Oakland hotel.

The cause of the fire has never been precisely identified, but the spreading speed has never been contested. The absence of a fire retardant sprinkler system made containment impossible. Faulty and uninspected wiring compounded by the stress imposed from music amplifiers may have been the cause. The dead had no outlet for escape from the flames or smoke inhalation.

Following two years of finger pointing and blame, the case evolved into criminal negligence. The focal point for blame became Derick Almena. He has done little to aid his credibility. In fact, he has essentially done everything conceivably wrong since the catastrophe.

During his initial public statements following the disaster, he expressed sadness for the destruction of the building and his *dream* art cooperative. He neglected to mention mourning for the thirty-six deaths or assume the slightest responsibility. Over the next three years, instead of expressing genuine humility or empathy, he has been combative and defiant casting himself as a victim. For the families and friends of the thirty-six casualties, such self-absorption is unforgivable.

Much has been written about his manipulation tactics and essential greed employed towards tenants. He has become the ideal villain. Is this designated role fair, criminal or even accurate?

His perceived emotional indifference and obstinacy singled him out in a greater proportion than others from a substantial pool of foils. His later expressed public sympathy for the victims has been perceived as insincere and self-serving. To date, Oakland city building, fire and law enforcement inspectors along with building owner Chor Ng have been spared legal accountability for their negligence

In 2018, Almena and Harris pleaded *no contest* to 36 counts of *involuntary manslaughter*. Under the terms of the accompanying agreement, Almena would have been sentenced to nine years and Harris six years in prison. The presiding judge scrapped the deal citing that Almena did not accept *full responsibility and remorse* for the fire. This reversal directly affected Harris who had expressed genuine remorse according to the judge. He was dragged into the morass further with a subsequent 2019 trial since the plea bargain arrangement was a package deal.

The 2019 trial has proven itself a fiasco of tragic and irresponsible proportions. On the tenth day of jury deliberations, three jurors were dismissed due to misconduct. Two allegedly were involved with a text media leak and the other for knowing and not reporting it. Three alternate jurors were transferred into the jury box leaving only one alternate remaining. On September 5, 2019 to the

218

horror of the victim's friends and families, Max Harris was acquitted of all charges and the jury could not unanimously convict Almena resulting in a hung jury. He will be tried individually in a subsequent trial. Both men will likely have civil charges files against them.

The lack of closure after nearly three years has proven unbearable and utterly unacceptable to all parties. What is certain is that 36 individuals perished in a preventable disaster. No one has assumed responsibility and no one involved has emerged from the ashes looking anything but charred.

Ghost Ship Warehouse Fire:
1305 31st Avenue, Oakland

Berkeley's Henry's Pub Hostage Nightmare

Shortly after midnight on September 28, 1990, 31-year-old Mehrdad Dashti, strolled into the popular Henry's Publick House and Grille located at the Hotel Durant (renamed in 2017 as the Graduate Berkeley Hotel) near the UC Berkeley campus. Dashti, originally born in Iran brought three weapons into the bar: a revolver and two pistols, one of them a fully automatic MAC-10, capable of firing a clip of 30 rounds at one time.

Dashti's original intentions were unclear but within a half hour he held 33 patrons and employees hostage. The perpetrator had arrived in the United States eight years previously and held a series of odd jobs. His fascination for weapons resulted in a large cache being stored in his apartment closet.

His erratic behavior had prompted the Alameda County Department of Social Services to classify him as a *paranoid schizophrenic*. He was responsible for writing a series of delusional but non-threatening letters to public officials and was the subject of a fraud investigation by San Francisco police, who suspected him of cashing $16,000 in stolen checks.

For seven agonizing hours he terrorized his captives ranting over a variety of sexual, racial and degrading subjects. He ordered all of the blond female hostages to undress below the waist and then labeled them *sluts and whores*. His behavior was described as a man in the midst of a *psychotic episode*.

Police negotiators unsuccessfully tried to disarm Dashti, communicating with him via telephone through a student hostage. During the course of these discussions, police were plotting the most expedient and safe course to storm the bar. When they concluded that the hostages were at one end of the bar and Dashti at the other, six armed officers charged into the facility. The gunman immediately shot out the light fixtures scattering flying glass.

Amidst the subsequent gunfire and confusion, hostages scattered to the streets, many crawling through the debris on their hands and knees. A firefight followed killing one hostage, John Sheehy, shot at close range. Six other students and one policeman were wounded by gunfire. Officers eventually killed Dashti with a stream of bullets to his head and chest.

**Harry's Bar at the Former Hotel Durant:
2600 Durant Avenue, Berkeley**

Port Costa and Still Living Cadavers

Port Costa is a living ruin of a town once integral to the transcontinental railroad. Upon the construction of the Carquinez (now called Al Zampa) and Martinez Bridges in the late 1930s, the train ferries servicing Port Costa were no longer essential for passenger or cargo transfers across the Carquinez Straights. As the port's significance diminished, so did the town's population, dwindling to approximately 100 people.

Access to Port Costa is limited to the winding Carquinez Scenic Drive roadway. The circuitous route features stunning views of forests, hills, valleys and seashore, but can be treacherous during inclement weather.

Arriving into the town, scattered houses line the main promenade leading to a diminutive commercial district consisting of a few boutique shops, a warehouse café (inside an enormous former grain warehouse) and the Burlington Hotel. The warehouse café is renowned for its libations bar, eclectic furnishings and murky lobster tank stocked and visible to patrons.

The 19-room Victorian Burlington Hotel was established in 1883 servicing a carousel of personalities including dockhands, adventurers, prostitutes, artists, partiers and contemporary hipsters. Each room was named after a woman, which may explain its former bordello reputation. Historic Port Costa was rampant with crime, gambling and whoring. The solitary Hotel Burlington was the vortex of activity.

The interior has been tidied up and the hallways and staircase are no longer immediately accessible from the streetfront. This reformed matron has regained her respectability, but cosmetics may only mask engrained age lines. In such a community of memories, the adjacent Carquinez Straits, part of the San Pablo Bay, supports numerous.

Creeping westward along the coast towards Crockett, a sunken former paddlewheel gambling boat, burned to cinders offshore. Its remains lie buried in the muck and eroding waters. Its name is obscured with the exception of a bronze memorial plaque stationed near the railroad tracks.

In 1889, on a wheat barge anchored off Benicia across the straits, *Gentleman* Jim Corbett, future Heavyweight Boxing Champion, fought Joe Choynski. The barge was positioned on the Contra Costa and Solano County border since prize fighting was illegal in California, but not apparently its waters. Benicia was notorious for their racetrack, cock fighting and duck shooting off the roof from one of the town's better brothels.

It was also the adopted home of cult hero John C. Heenan, known as the *Benicia Boy*, originally from Troy, New York. Heenan was one of the best-known American boxers before John L. Sullivan. In 1860, the 190-pound bare-knuckled fighter battled British champion Tom Sayers in Farnborough, England. This was his second formal bout following an initial loss.

In the heat of combat, Sayers launched a crushing left to Heenan's forehead opening a bleeding gash that partially blinded him. The result was Heenan decked two of Sayers' seconds and three nearby spectators. Further enraged, he attempted to strangle Sayers on the ring ropes until prevented by several English partisans separating the two. The referee had vanished earlier for a drink or perhaps an entire bottle. He returned to the chaos to declare the fight a draw, probably averting a riot.

Heenan returned to England to battle the new British Champion, Tom King. He fared worse this time losing decisively. His final professional boxing record ended at 0-2-1.

Amidst the Crockett docklands lays a protruding wreck of the *S. S. Garden City*, a former wooden paddlewheel steamboat. The boilers and paddle wheel hub remain following a 1983 fire that destroyed the nearby ferry terminal. Built in 1879, the *Garden City* was 208 feet long, weighted 1,080 tons was operated by a crew of 19 men. The steamboat ferried passengers and automobiles across the Carquinez Straits.

The silent waters betray minimal history. Port Costa remains isolated and the Burlington Hotel is rumored to be haunted. The town has escaped with its life the contemporary rush towards modernity and real estate speculation. It prefers being historically forgotten and savored for its timelessness.

Hotel Burlington: 2 Canyon Lake Drive, Port Costa

Huey P. Newton: A Tarnished Messenger with Feet of Clay

On the morning of August 22, 1989 at approximately 5:15 a.m., Huey P. Newton's life ended abruptly on a sidewalk in the Lower Bottoms neighborhood of West Oakland. Newton, the self-titled Minister of Defense for the militant Black Panther Party of Oakland met his ignominious death with certainty. He resolutely faced his killer, half his age. He probably understood at that instant the cycle of violent confrontation he had publicly espoused would ultimately claim his own life.

Various media accounts melodramatically reported that he taunted his murderer Tyrone Robinson by quoting prophetically, *You can kill my body, and you can take my life but you can never kill my soul. My soul will live forever!* Robinson responded by shooting him point blank multiple times in the face. Newton, the enigmatic messenger was dispassionately erased from the streets of his adopted Oakland.

The 1400 block of Ninth Street, the crime scene, was not Newton's Oakland residential neighborhood. He frequented the vice-plagued area habitually. Decaying but statuesque Victorian houses visually softened the prevalent drug trade and prostitution. As neighborhood residents related in published reports then, one sealed their front doors when the evening gunshots echoed into the darkness.

Over twenty-five years later, real estate speculation has superficially freshened and gentrified the neighborhood. The effect has not eradicated the shadows of a violent past. One does not linger or loiter in this neighborhood without consequence.

Newton's fate was prompted by a chance encounter following his exit from a Ninth Street crack cocaine house. Tyrone Robinson, then twenty-four years old was already an ex-convict and reputed drug dealer. He was a member of the *Black Guerrilla Family*, a prison gang founded in 1966 by George Jackson while he was incarcerated at San Quentin. Jackson had met his own violent demise at San Quentin and his attempted release was the motivation for the 1970 Marin County Courthouse shootout.

Robinson claimed Newton's killing was self-defense, maintaining that the victim had pulled a gun on him demanding cocaine when the two converged on a nearby street corner. Newton's gun was never recovered.

Robinson was convicted of the murder in 1991 and sentenced to 32 years in prison. He began his sentence at San Quentin and was later transferred to Pelican Bay, then Corcoran and currently at the California State Prison in Sacramento, obscured and disregarded. He added the name Kambui to his in 2016. His identity and role were inconvenient aspects of the martyrdom that would later shroud Newton's mythology. His role has become largely antidotal over twenty-five years after the act. He has participated in three prison hunger strikes between 2011-2013 and joined an organization called the *New Afrikan Revolutionary Nationalism Collective Think Tank*.

Huey Newton was cremated and his ashes reportedly interred at Evergreen Cemetery in Oakland, the same location where 412 unclaimed bodies of the Jonestown mass suicide are buried. Various interpretations of his life and struggles have been reinvented and interpreted for iconic literature, cinema and political commentary involving American race relations. The reality of his life and actions are far more complicated.

Was he a legitimate freedom fighter or simply a sociopathic street thug repeating revolutionary slogans he had not authored?

Newton served as a willing symbol for the radical Black Panther Party, a group he co-founded while still a student at Merritt College in October of 1966. Newton epitomized the best and worst elements of the social consciousness movement. Charismatic, charming and articulate, his forceful personality energized a movement bent on confrontation.

The Black Panther Party became an armed political organization oriented towards African-American rights. Discarding the non-violent protest tactics of the southern Civil Rights movement, the Panthers advocated that violence and/or its impending threat would expedite social change.

Their leadership from its inception understood the propaganda impact of media manipulation and public spectacle. A contingent of Black Panthers once entered the California Legislature chambers fully armed in order to protest a gun bill being debated. Their on-site street provocations included interrupting arrests and other police activities when they presumed that African-American citizens were being intimidated. Their organizational leaders and members were targeted, harassed and under regular surveillance by law enforcement authorities.

The tenor of the times and mutual provocation ultimately provoked violence between the Panthers and law enforcement agencies. Newton's destructive seeds were sewn deeply. He exhibited violent tendencies and reckless impulsive behavior behind his flamboyant public veneer.

Death accompanied his turbulent cult of personality in the form of inconvenient witnesses, peers and street acquaintances. The most prominent homicide was his voluntary manslaughter conviction of Oakland Policeman John Frey in 1968. Frey was killed while arresting Newton, shot with his own gun. The responsible weapon was never located.

Newton's repeated altercations with the legal system, his peers and stretches of imprisonment become depressing reading. He chose exile in Havana, Cuba between 1974-77 due to pending murder and assault charges against him. He returned to imprisonment and public trial. A succession of mistrials released him but his social consciousness rhetoric became perceived as opportunistic and insincere. In 1982, Newton was accused and tried on embezzlement charges involving a Black Panther founded Oakland Community School. He pleaded no contest to a single allegation and served a six-month jail term.

The vibrancy and urgency of violent racial militancy waned by the conclusion of the 1970's. The movement had disintegrated into contending factions and the founding Black Panther Party was disbanded in 1982. The leadership abuses had undermined the constructive community works of the party.

During the final year of Newton's unraveling life, he spent 90 days incarcerated at San Quentin Prison for possessing drug paraphernalia, a violation of his parole from one of his earlier cases. The climatic confrontation on Ninth Street seemed inevitable. His narcissism, personal demons and downward personality spiral had already sabotaged his social change relevance.

Today, a solitary sapling and handicapped parking sign identify Newton's earthly exit. When viewed from the east, the trees shadow resembles a prone and sprawled body silhouette. From whatever prism one views Newton's legacy, his death became another senseless urban casualty. An estimated 1000+ mourners at his Allen Temple Baptist Church funeral service lavished accolades and tributes upon him one week following his murder. The forgotten and dishonored prophet was resurrected as an icon of the protest idealism of the 1960s and 70s.

Huey P. Newton, the deeply flawed, charismatic and intelligent individual becomes indecipherable. Twenty-five years later, the measure of his influence remains as elusive as our full understanding of the protest era. Time and perspective may one day make coherent sense of the period and the man.

Huey Newton Murder Site:
1400 Block of Ninth Street, Oakland

Laci Peterson: When Motive Convicts Beyond the Body of Evidence

On April 13, 2003, a couple walking their dog in Point Isabel State Park found a male fetus on the sands. The next day, the body of a pregnant woman washed ashore amidst the jagged stones nearby and was discovered by another dog-walker. The bodies were decomposed and hers was decapitated. DNA tests verified that they were the bodies of Laci Peterson and her yet born son, Conner.

The discovery ended a highly publicized hunt for the pair. Laci became the subject of a murder case after she went missing while seven and a half months pregnant with her only child. She was reportedly last seen alive on December 24, 2002. Law enforcement authorities already suspected her husband Scott of the being responsible for the murder. The finding of the bodies enabled prosecutors to formally press charges against him five days later.

Although the point at which both bodies washed up was approximately 90 miles from the couple's home, the site was a mere 5 miles from the Berkeley Marina where Scott had said he'd gone fishing the morning of Christmas Eve.

Scott Peterson was arrested on April 18, 2003 in La Jolla, California in the parking lot of a golf course. He claimed to be meeting his father and brother for a round of golf. At the time of his arrest, he was reportedly carrying $15,000 in cash, four cell phones, camping equipment, a gun, his brother's driver's license and 12 tablets of Viagra. His hair and goatee had been beached blond. Police speculated his intention might have been to flee to Mexico, where extradition procedures are complicated. As with all of his other schemes, the plan was poorly thought out and executed.

Scott and Laci Peterson resembled a happy young couple with good jobs, two nice cars, and a new house of their own in Modesto. The relationships between their families and in-laws were warm and they were about to have a baby.

For Scott, his marriage was a façade masking deeper anxieties. He was worried about his job performance and about turning 30. Scott was reported to have told anyone who'd listen that he wasn't comfortable with his impending fatherhood. The couple was living beyond their financial means.

Assuming responsibility for his unhappiness, he could have left his wife and child. The consequences, however, would have probably saddled him with alimony and child support payments.

Instead of getting a divorce, court evidence indicted that he began to assemble a new identity and lifestyle persona. He took out a substantial life insurance policy on his wife. He planned her false kidnapping and murder while providing himself an alibi by taking a solo fishing trip on the day she would disappear.

His plan initially appeared solid, as his in-laws were very supportive of him in the beginning. Over time, the farce and flimsiness of his plot became evident. The disclosure of a mistress and his repeated deceptions and lying to all parties involved with the case, cracked any solidarity or empathy towards him and his plight. All that was lacking was a body and a murder weapon to put him on trial.

A massive citywide search effort and $500,000 reward for any information leading to Laci Peterson's safe return yielded nothing. Over 1,000 volunteers signed up to distribute information and to help search for her. Many observed that Scott Peterson's direct involvement seemed detached, remote and distant from the proceedings.

The bodies washed ashore, despite the killer's resolute efforts to keep them permanently submerged. Their discovery sealed his fate. His trial ran from June 2004 through March 2005 with enormous national press coverage. Peterson's defense team repeatedly tried to discredit any suggestion of motive and even formulated a fanciful theory about Laci's kidnapping being the work of a cult.

The jury rejected their arguments and reasoning. Motive and Peterson's pattern of suspicious behavior ultimately became the swaying factor towards their decision. Physical evidence was almost non-existent with the exception of traces of Laci's hair in his boat.

The jury deliberated for seven days before convicting Scott Peterson of murder in the first degree for Laci's death, and in the second degree for the death of their prenatal son, Conner. He was sentenced to death row at San Quentin State Prison where he is currently interned. The excessive exposure of the trial and legal grandstanding probably backfired for Peterson and contributed to his maximum sentence.

Laci Peterson suffered a cruel and callous death. As an innocent participant in Scott Peterson's fantasized love triangle, she paid exceedingly for her fidelity. The motive for her killing eventually emerged as obvious as the incompetence and deceit her husband played in the tragic drama.

Laci Peterson Murder:
523 Covena Avenue, Modesto

Laci and Connor Peterson's Dead Body Discovery:
Point Isabel State Park, 2701 Isabel Street, Richmond

Lovelle Mixon: A Desperate Final and Fatal Gamble Towards Escape

Commuters daily pass a highway sign on Interstate 580 daily with minimal regard. The memorial eulogizes Oakland Motorcycle Sergeant Mark Dunakin (40), Motorcycle Officer John Hege (41), SWAT Sergeant Ervin Romans (43) and SWAT Sergeant Daniel Sakai (35) killed by a convicted felon.

Their murders equaled the single deadliest attack on California police offers since the Newhall massacre in 1970 when four California Highway Patrol officers were shot and killed by two men in Newhall.

On Saturday, March 21, 2009 at 1:00 p.m. Lovelle Mixon's 1995 Buick Sedan was pulled over by officers Dunakin and Hege for a routine traffic violation on the 7400 block of MacArthur Boulevard.

Mixon had multiple reasons for concern besides a simple citation. The driver's license he produced for Dunakin was fake and he was wanted on a no-bail warrant for a parole violation. Seven hours before, he had raped two women at gunpoint in another sector of East Oakland.

Dunakin suspected the license was fraudulent and signaled for his partner to arrest Mixon. Whether or not Mixon noticed the gesture couldn't be determined. He leaned out of the vehicle's passenger side window and opened fire on both with a 9mm semiautomatic pistol. He methodically wounded both officers twice, exited his vehicle and approached each. He finished them off execution style in the back. After admiring his handiwork, he fled southbound on foot.

Both officers had died before the ambulances arrived. The manhunt to apprehend Mixon was immediate and involved over 200 officers from various law enforcement agencies throughout the county.

Mixon didn't have time to escape far and chose the most predictable destination, his sister's apartment one-block down the street. He was spotted entering the two-bedroom ground level apartment. A SWAT team was immediately ordered to surround the building.

Unknown to them, Mixon had secured an SKS carbine presumably stored within his sister's apartment. The lead officers present concluded that other building residents were at severe risk should they be forced to evacuate through a single front building entry door. The same officers were also suspicious over the credibility of the eyewitnesses.

Rather than wait for a full SWAT team to assemble or simply surround the apartment and delay, a decision was made to storm the unit. The decision proved premature and fatally flawed.

Mixon had barricaded himself in his sister's bedroom, which was poorly illuminated. Shock flashbang grenades that were tossed in by the approaching police team created more confusion. As the initial SWAT team members broke down the front door and entered, Mixon ambushed them. Sergeant Pat Gonzales, the first assault member was wounded in the shoulder and Sergeant Romans following him was mortally wounded.

In the ensuing firefight, SWAT member Sakai was killed and Mixon ultimately felled by a barrage of gunfire. The raid lasted less than fifteen minutes.

The history of Lovelle Mixon's brief life makes gloomy reading. At the age of 13, his antisocial behavior had manifested itself through multiple assault and battery occurrences. At 20, he was convicted for felony assault with a deadly weapon stemming from an armed robbery in San Francisco. He served six years at Corcoran State Prison. Upon his release, he violated the terms of his parole and was returned for another nine months.

No one could accuse him of ignorance towards the consequences of parole violation.

Yet even Satan has his advocates. Mixon's family vehemently protested that he was not a monster. One member indicated his latest parole violation stemmed from a feud he was having with his parole agent. Mixon was angered that his agent had missed earlier appointments. Mixon chose to miss subsequent mandatory sessions in protest.

The future for Lovelle Mixon was not encouraging based on his precedent behavior. Redemption and reform did not appear to be his personal priority. Two months following his death, DNA evidence positively linked him to another rape of a 12-year-old.

Understanding the actions of a desperate man driven to extremes is not difficult. Recognizing that our criminal justice system cannot contain violent felons such as Mixon keeps everyone at risk. For Mixon, there will be no public trial, condemnation by jury, contrition or apologies by him to the widow and grieving families.

The trade of four vital law enforcement officers for one utterly insignificant felon proved a poor exchange for society.

Lovelle Mixon Traffic Stop:
7400 Block of MacArthur Boulevard, East Oakland

Oaks Card Club: Historic Gaming Surviving Amidst an Expansive Environment

Opened in 1890, the Oaks Card Club has remained an enduring and solitary legacy of a town once labeled a *modern-day Gomorrah* in 1925. Emeryville was reputed for its debauchery and packed with speakeasies, bootlegger barns, a dog racetrack (near Shellmound Park), brothels, saloons and an abundance of gambling and loan sharking establishments. The Pacific Coast League Oakland Oaks baseball team played nearby in their 11,000-seat Oaks Park between 1913-1955.

City government and law enforcement were notably corrupt. Mobsters such as Lucky Luciano's *La Costa Nosta* had firmly established local operations. The police department operated the local liquor delivery fleet during the Prohibition Era. The city reportedly did not construct its first church until the 1960s.

The city's biggest nemesis during the 1920s was Alameda District Attorney Earl Warren who unsuccessfully attempted to clean up the profitable gambling and bootlegging operations. Warren would later be appointed to the United States Supreme Court and swear in President John F. Kennedy at his 1960 inauguration.

The Oaks Card Room is last of ten formerly operating card rooms that sprang up around the dog racetrack. Their operation is distinguished by only offering card games between players playing against themselves and not again the *House*. They feature no slot machines, roulette or other popular Casino games of chance.

Emeryville has evolved into a contemporary shopping hub and crucial high-rise living destination for East Bay and

San Francisco based employees. Tech, biotech and small industrial warehouses form the core of planned urban renewal. Amidst the ambitious strategies for modernization, the Oaks Card Room remains a landmark of longevity surviving even an economic *laissez-faire* era showcasing its worst excesses.

Oaks Card Club:
4907 San Pablo Avenue, Emeryville

The Oikos University Massacre: Piecing Together a Disjointed Puzzle

The underlying reasons behind rampage killings are often difficult to pinpoint. The tragic results frequently end with a self-inflicted suicide by the killers and no answers.

It is left for the media, law enforcement officials, survivors and their families to piece together explanatory motives of apparent senseless acts. The disintegration of a killer's personality and orderly identity may appear obvious in retrospect. Behind each perpetrator is a human being that was either a simmering psychopath or a tormented individual that concluded they could no longer exist or tolerate their living environment.

Does conceptually understanding the devil's motives make his atrocities less despicable?

One L. Goh does not easily classify into the definition of student rampage killer, even given the setting of his shooting spree, an educational institution. American schools have become a depressingly recurring setting for mass shootings. The motives vary, but the shooters are typically male, adolescent and fringe members of their student bodies.

At approximately 10:30 a.m. on April 2, 2012, Goh, 43, entered an Oikos University nursing class in session, lined up its students against a wall and began firing a .45-caliber semi-automatic handgun. His aim was predominantly towards female students. He killed seven and wounded another three students. Oikos University is a Korean Christian college located in a business park nearby the Oakland International Airport. The campus resembles one of the expansive wholesale and product distribution warehouses that populate the neighborhood.

Oikos offers credentials in Christian Theology, Music and Nursing, the degree he briefly pursued earlier during the 2012 Spring Semester. He had dropped out of the program after only a few months. Other sources had him expelled for unspecified disciplinary reasons. He became bitter over his departure and the school's refusal to refund him full or even partial tuition monies. The administrator, who was identified as his most likely target, publicly disputed the allegation. She maintained that he had *voluntarily* left the program on his own. The issue of accuracy may or may not be resolved during his impending court trial.

Dismissing his actions as straightforward mania becomes simplistic. In the eyes of the grieving innocent victim's families, there can normally be no alternative. Their profound grief attached to the loss of their loved ones leaves little space for compassion towards a cold-blooded executioner. Through most eyes, his acts were wrong, unconscionable and premeditated. Through most eyes, the culprit should be duly punished.

The sole question remaining is whether he receives a capital punishment sentence or will be permanently confined to a California mental institution.

Goh was a native of South Korea and followed his parents and two older brothers to the United States during his youth, later becoming a U.S. citizen. He initially resided in Virginia, just outside of Washington D.C. and then relocated to the rural southwestern portion of the state. He helped run a construction company until mid-2008.

The construction industry splintered nationally and collapsed with the widespread housing meltdown. By the summer of 2008, Goh had lost his income, was evicted from his apartment and creditors impounded his car. He ended up living with his father in Oakland at a housing project for senior citizens. He worked at a San Mateo warehouse, with his father at a Daly City grocery store and periodically as a mover. He had not yet surrendered hope to his diminishing prospects.

Contemporary American culture promotes an obsessive notion over the necessity of sustained forward progress or reinvention. Anything less is perceived as failure. Viewing habitually the garish displays of wealth in the Bay Area can be a disillusioning barometer for the legions that have failed to keep pace.

Goh's financial disasters were compounded by family calamity. In 2011, his most favored brother, an Iraq War veteran and decorated Special Forces hero died in a freak head-on collision with a multi-ton boulder stationary on a Virginia road traveling at 70 mph. The news devastated his family and especially his mother. She returned to Korea and died only months after his brother's funeral.

Goh's father supplemented his son's attempt at reinvention with a $6,000 loan to pay for his Oikos nursing tuition. The investment proved disappointing with Goh's abrupt departure from the school. Numerous published reports confirmed he was widely teased for his advanced age, chubby appearance and poor English skills. Persistent bullying and physiological harassment are common ignition triggers for rampage killings.

Disillusionment with his choice of school may have influenced his decision to leave, assuming he did so voluntarily. Examining reports have condemned Oikos substandard academic and job placement track record. Was his shooting decision influenced by a bitter realization that he had chosen the wrong vehicle for redemption?

A single, several or all of these factors may have accumulated to make One L. Goh snap. His career transformation project had clearly failed with his departure from the school. Had he reached the identical dead-end conclusion many irate shooters share in common?

In the attempted analysis to understand an evil act, it is convenient but negligent to forget the victims. Killed were Tshering Rinzing Bhutia (38), Doris Chibuko (40), Sonam Chodon (33), Grace Eunhae Kim (23), Katleen Ping (24), Judith Seymour (53) and Lydia Sim (21). Wounded were Dawinder Kaur (19), Grace Kirika (43) and Ahmad Javid Sayeed (36). Were any of his victims also his tormenters or merely the random targets of his rage?

He surrendered several hours after the shootings approximately five miles away in an Alameda Safeway parking lot without resistance.

One L. Goh clearly suffered a concentrated accumulation of reverses. Judging his mental stability and motivations are further complicated by his inability to articulate using the English language. During his upcoming trial, should it ever occur, a third-party defense team will likely distribute blame and responsibility elsewhere.

Even they may never share a public forum to vent specific causes and effect.

His setbacks however are not necessarily unique. Many individuals who've suffered worse misfortunes have coped, re-grouped and recovered in varying degrees based on their resiliency. Their struggles do not generate headline news or prompt violent expression.

Goh was arraigned two days following the murders and was charged with seven counts of murder and three counts of attempted murder. He did not enter a plea.

In jailhouse media interviews, he followed a more conventional response tactic by indicating he was *deeply sorry* for the killings, but only remembered parts of the day. Amnesia and short-term memory loss consistently plague numerous murderers performing heinous acts.

Following his initial court appearance and interviews, he went on a hunger strike losing twenty pounds. He resumed eating after forced feeding intervention was threatened and later that month at a second hearing, pleaded not guilty.

His path towards public accountability has followed a labyrinth following a November 2012 hearing to determine his competency to stand trial. He was diagnosed with paranoid schizophrenia, which made cooperation with his appointed public defender impossible based on his apparent incomprehension with the criminal justice system. During the trial, Goh was assigned a Korean translator. He briefly disrupted the proceedings once with an outburst when his defense attorney was discussing his mental competence.

During a third January 2013 hearing, a second psychiatrist's report re-confirmed the identical initial diagnosis. Goh reportedly has refused all medication while incarcerated and has been reportedly forcibly medicated. In a December 2015 hearing, an Alameda County Superior Court Judge ruled him *incompetent* to stand trial for murder. At that hearing, Goh expressed his wish for the death penalty as he had on many occasions previously.

While his case languished in uncertainty, Goh was confined to Napa State Hospital, a mental institution for treatment and subsequent competency reviews. In April 2017, Goh was finally declared *competent for trial*.

He pleaded *no contest* in May 2017 and accepted a plea deal. He was sentenced to seven consecutive life sentences plus 271 years in prison without any possibility of parole. His sentence was terminated abruptly when he died on March 29, 2019, while in custody at the California State Prison in Sacramento.

Throughout nearly seven years of waiting for closure, the three survivors and victim's families have attempted to reattach their own disjointed puzzles. Goh's sudden and *wished-for* death became a further plunge into the darkness of the unexplainable.

Oikos University Massacre:
7850 Edgewater Drive, Oakland

Oscar Grant III: When The Facts Behind a Killing Become Secondary

Oscar Grant III was a 22 year-old father when he was fatally shot by BART (Bay Area Rapid Transit District) police officer Johannes Mehserle at approximately 2:00 a.m. on New Year's Day 2009. The altercation was precipitated by six officers responding to reports of a fight on a crowded BART train returning from San Francisco. Police officers detained Grant and approximately a dozen other passengers on the platform at the Oakland Fruitvale Station based on the complaint.

The ensuing New Years Eve chaos created a hostile and explosive environment for the officers once they removed the offending passengers from the train. Insults and aggressive behavior were traded. The removed passengers were seated against a station wall. Mehserle and another officer were restraining Grant, who was lying face down and refusing to submit to handcuffing. According to Mehserle during testimony, Grant was reaching for his waistband where he sensed perhaps a handgun might be hidden.

In response, Mehserle drew his gun, a SIG Sauer P226 and shot Grant once in the back. Grant was unarmed. He was pronounced dead the next morning at Highland Hospital in Oakland. Mehserle insisted that he was reaching for his Taser and pulled out the heavier gun in error. The events were captured on multiple digital video and cell phone cameras. The footage was distributed to media outlets and websites worldwide, where millions watched it.

The killing was magnified because Grant was African-American and Mehserle, Caucasian. The following days witnessed protests in downtown Oakland. Initial daytime protests against the ruling were peacefully organized. Looting, arson, destruction of property and small riots broke out after dark. Nearly 80 people were eventually arrested.

The shooting has been variously labeled as accidental or an impulsive execution depending upon ones perspective.

American society has yet to fully resolve and bury its persisting racial divide. Tragedies as these become divisive issues to stir old wounds and provide forums for self-serving interests and causes. The continuing financial gulf and perceived inequity between social classes habitually raises the thorny issues of racial inequality. Grant's death served as a pretext to rekindle the debate between the haves and have-nots.

No direct evidence or public admission by Mehserle's suggested that his action was racially motivated. Yet in the eyes of many professional activists and protestors, the skin difference between the two men was sufficient.

On January 30, 2010, Alameda County prosecutors charged Mehserle with murder for the shooting. He resigned his law enforcement position and pleaded not guilty. Slightly over six months later, a jury found Mehserle guilty of involuntary manslaughter and not guilty of second-degree murder and voluntary manslaughter. He was sentenced to two years, minus time served. He served his time in the Los Angeles County Jail, occupying a private cell away from other prisoners. He was released on May 3, 2011.

Several wrongful death claims were filed against the publicly funded transit district. BART settled with Grant's daughter and mother for a total of $2.8 million in 2011.

A killing under these extreme circumstances provokes the eternal question as to true motive.

Was Mehserle simply incompetent and emotionally overwhelmed by firing his handgun amidst the chaos of events? Or was his act a simple execution because he had been pushed over the edge by taunting? We cannot truly know his intention but the act ruined his livelihood and reputation. It will remain his lifelong epitaph and trail him the rest of his life.

The act itself cost Oscar Grant III his life.

Sometimes in society's search for clarity, reason prevails. Too often this search is drowned out by conflicting voices. The actual details behind the tragedy became secondary in many people's eyes. The racial implications attached to the case clearly tinted the facts and the perception of each party's responsibility.

We must continually ask who is ultimately responsible for dispensing justice in our society? At what point must individuals assume responsibility for their actions and direct challenge to authority? In Grant's case, his actions clearly contributed to the tragic and lethal consequences.

We ask many things of our law enforcement community. We demand their instantaneous discernment in manners of conflict and crisis. We insist that they shield and protect the victimized while bringing accountability to their perpetrators. We assume their actions will reflect fair judgment despite harassment, antagonism and often indifference.

What happens to these expectations when their actions become deflected by circumstance or their own flawed decision-making? Are they allowed to be human and make errors?

The consequences of Mehserle's instantaneous act became a lifelong stain for all involved parties. The condemnation and blame unfortunately will never be commuted nor resolved.

Oscar Grant III Killing:
Fruitvale BART Station Upper Platform
3401 East 12th Street, Oakland

The Patty Hearst Kidnapping: The Final Nail into the Coffin of Idealism

The kidnapping and subsequent odyssey of Patricia Hearst began on the evening of February 4, 1974. A band of armed men and women knocked on her Berkeley apartment door and within minutes had abducted her, beaten up her fiancé and tossed her into their car truck. They then returned to their headquarters in a Western Addition apartment in San Francisco.

Their 19-year old victim was no average UC Berkeley college student. She was the granddaughter and heiress of publisher William Randolph Hearst.

The kidnapping elevated the status of a group of armed idealists, named the Symbionese Liberation Army (SLA), led by an ex-con named Donald DeFreeze. Hearst's kidnapping was motivated by the group's need to erase the memory of their only known activity up to that time. In November of 1973, the SLA had callously and stupidly murdered Dr. Marcus Foster, the Oakland Superintendent of Schools and seriously wounded his assistant with cyanide-tipped bullets. Two of their shooters were in custody for the murder.

The SLA was an extremist group loaded with guns and rhetoric and an ability to milk media exposure with empty clichéd ideology. Their ranks included both genders, blacks and whites, anarchists and idealists from diverse walks of life.

The SLA had significant propaganda plans for Patty Hearst. After all, what could be more potent to their revolutionary cause than the successful recruitment of an heiress from the

260

elite establishment? Their stated goals included an overthrow of contemporary society.

But first, they had to brainwash and destroy any potential resistance by her.

By her account, she was clandestinely housed in a Golden Gate Avenue apartment building in San Francisco. Hearst was blindfolded and isolated in a third floor closet for two months, oblivious to the enormous media frenzy stimulated by her kidnapping. She was repeatedly abused and violated mentally, physically and emotionally. Acceptance and cooperation with their agenda became her sole possibility of survival.

Their brainwashing techniques worked. Hearst was coerced into making inflammatory statements against her family and those she had been closest to before her kidnapping. She integrated seamlessly into SLA operations and ultimately participated in an armed bank robbery in the Sunset district of San Francisco. While captive, the SLA made extravagant ransom requests of her father including demands for distributing millions of dollars in free food to the poor. This audacious stipulation turned into a fiasco with much of the inventory being stolen and disappearing without any form of accountability.

Patty Hearst proved too valuable for the group to release, but their own fate was nearing a violent conclusion. While relatively secure within the Bay Area due to an abundance of safe houses, DeFreeze impulsively opted to shift his operations to Los Angeles. This decision became their undoing.

An unsuccessful petty shoplifting debacle traced the group's van to their temporary residence. The following day on May 17, the Los Angeles police surrounded the house. A massive fuselage followed. Law enforcement officers showed little interest in taking prisoners once they were fired upon. The building went up in flames. Six members of the SLA died in the blaze, including DeFreeze who shot himself fatally while simultaneously on fire.

The site of the destroyed house remained a vacant lot for decades. Today it integrates into the existing neighborhood seemingly buried amidst abundant landscaping foliage

Hearst was not involved in the South Central Los Angeles firefight as she and other members were holed up in an Anaheim hotel room. The remaining SLA gang returned to northern California and disbanded around the country to avoid captures. Hearst was arrested on September 18 and charged with multiple counts including bank robbery.

The judicial circus that followed raised legal liability issues regarding illegal activities performed by forced coercion and brainwashing. Did Hearst fabricate her treatment by the SLA to avoid severe consequences for her actions? There was little doubt that she was unwillingly kidnapped but only Patty Hearst and remaining SLA survivors can attest to the truth towards her subsequent activities and motivations.

The jury at her trial discarded her brainwashing defense. She was found guilty and sentenced to seven years in prison, for which she served two. President Jimmy Carter commuted her sentence and she was later pardoned.

The Heart kidnapping was symptomatic of arguably the most turbulent era of social hostility in San Francisco's history. The abandonment of the peace and love idealism from the prior decade had been eclipsed by a cycle of violence that would haunt the city for the remainder of the decade.

**Patty Hearst Kidnapping Site:
2603 Benvenue Street #4, Berkeley**

Patty Hearst Kidnapping Safe House:
1827 Golden Gate Avenue San Francisco

SLA Bank Robbery:
Hibernia Bank: 1450 Noriega Street San Francisco

SLA Shootout with Los Angeles Police:
1466 East 54th Street Los Angeles

Pleasanton Hotel: Alternating Naming Rights in a *Desperate* Town

The town of Pleasanton was originally named *Alisal* in the 1850s and nicknamed the *most desperate town in the West*. Gangs, bandits and drifters passed through and periodically skirmished with the locals. Debauchery, shoot outs and general mayhem typified this frontier settlement that has apparently tamed over the passing century. In the 1960s, *Life Magazine dubbed* the community *the drinking-est town in the United States* attributable to 19 bars alone located on Main Street

The current Pleasanton Hotel remains one of the few enduring landmarks of an unruly era. The *original* Pleasanton Hotel was constructed in 1863 on the site of a present day *Round Table Pizza*. When Jason Rose later bought the hotel, he changed the name to the *Rose Hotel*. Curiously a fresh three-story, 38-room *Rose Hotel* occupies 807 Main Street following its 2001 construction at the former St. Vincent de Paul building site.

The *Germania Hotel* located on Main Street renamed itself the *Pleasanton Hotel* until 1930 when the property burned down and replaced by a gas station. The Coast Gasoline station featured uniformed attendants that pumped gas, checked under the hood and washed each client's car windows. Further north up Main Street, the former *Farmer's Hotel* constructed in 1864 by John Kottinger assumed the name during the 1940s and so it has remained.

In 1898, the original *Farmer's Hotel* burned to the ground. A replacement was immediately constructed but in 1915, a second fire destroyed the dining room area in the rear of the property. In the late 1920s, the name of the hotel was the *Riverside Hotel*.

The neighborhood has a storied past of residences by bandit Joaquin Murrieta and gangster Mickey Cohen's brother who frequented poker games at the hotel property. A tunnel once connected the Pleasanton Hotel to Kottinger Barn, the city's lone historically registered structure. Others stretched along various segments of Main Street. They have essentially caved in or are occupied now by vermin.

The past has failed to entirely reconcile with the present. An unnamed prostitute stabbed to death in 1870 by a jealous client reportedly lurks in the hallways of the current Pleasanton Hotel. Her image has been captured on film conveniently during annual *Ghost Walks*. Her appearance seems only natural amidst a topography reeking with disorderly spirits.

Pleasanton Hotel:
855 Main Street, Pleasanton

Jockey Ron Hansen: Speed Killed

Swift living and riding jockey Ron Hanson was responsible for 3,700 career wins that earned in excess of $36 million. He was a leading fixture at the Bay Area's Golden Gate Fields and Bay Meadows racetracks between 1988-91 and rode *Video Ranger* to a fourth place finish in the 1990 Kentucky Derby despite 65-1 odds.

Hansen was popular amongst his peers and a noted storyteller who loved basking in attention. From tales of his future wife spitting on him during their first encounter following a losing mount to their La Vegas wedding ceremony in the nude, Hanson was not above exaggeration or embellishment.

Drinking was Hanson's Achilles heal which had the capacity to be hazardous to his professional health due to mandated Breathalyzer tests before rides. He had been previously banned from Golden Gate Fields briefly for suspected race fixing, but was exonerated when the allegations proved to be groundless.

On the evening of October 1, 1993 after having ridden eight races earlier at Bay Meadows, Hansen was spotted at 1 a.m. drinking at *The Van's Restaurant* nearby the track. He left their bar and drove to the nearby Hillsdale Inn, a motel with a bar. He telephoned his wife to indicate he would be crashing at a friend's apartment nearby since he was due at the track for early workouts the next morning.

At 2 a.m. Hansen left his friend's apartment supposedly to relocate his car to a proper parking space. From there, a mystery surrounding his whereabouts intensified.

At 2:30 a.m. Hansen's 1990 Jaguar XJS approached the

San Mateo Bridge at speeds as high as 100 mph heading east, possibly en route to his home in Alameda. Switching lanes, the Jaguar rear-ended another car. That vehicle crashed into the concrete bridge siding and flipped over.

Hansen's Jaguar was recovered a mile further on the span. Its hazard lights were flashing and his wallet still in the glove compartment. One witness viewed a man walking towards the east end of the bridge three quarters of a mile from the abandoned Jaguar.

Hanson failed to show up for both the morning workout and his scheduled ride later that afternoon which his horse won. For three months, he remained missing. Speculation ranged from his staging a disappearance to an organized crime killing. His wife, friends and associates remained baffled by his disappearance.

His remains were finally sighted by a passing truck driver in the sludge flats approximately ten feet from the east end of the bridge. Due to the body's decomposed state, he was officially identified through dental records. Suspicion was raised because the water is only two to eight feet deep at that end of the bridge. However, the mud has the same properties as quicksand and Hansen could have easily been stuck following an impulsive plunge into the waters, especially being inebriated.

In 1997, the FBI opened an investigation into racetrack irregularities and Hanson's death was re-investigated. Their findings prompted no subsequent action. No one will likely ever know the exact scenario behind his death. The most probable theory is that he panicked after the accident (the driver survived) and due to his drinking and speed, he vainly attempted to flee. His folly cost him his life at the age of 33

Ron Hansen's Body Discovery:
Adjacent to the east end of the San Mateo Bridge
(Hayward side)

Ted Kaczynski: To Arms Against A Faceless Society and Enemy

It is difficult to isolate the juncture where genius and madness intersect within a troubled personality. Once these paths have diverged, conventional understanding behind an individual's homicidal behavior becomes incomprehensible.

In theory, it is understandable that genius may not recuperate using traditional mental illness therapies and medications. A highly developed thinker rarely views the world through a mainstream perspective. The complexity and elevated rational capacity that ultimately separates genius may potentially alienate it from society.

Ted Kaczynski was a recognized mathematical genius but his legacy will remain as the *Unabomber Killer*. His mania was responsible for the death of three people and injury of 23 more before his arrest in 1996.

A high school academic prodigy, he was accepted to Harvard University in 1958 at the impressionable age of 16. While at Harvard, Kaczynski was taught by famed logician Willard Van Orman Quine, scoring at the top of his class. Dr. Henry Murray selected him amongst 22 other undergraduates as guinea pigs for a series of ethically questionable experiments. Murray subjected each of the participants to extreme stress levels including verbal abuse, personality attacks and complete disregard for their own their cherished belief system.

The focus of these aggressive studies was purportedly to measure participant's abilities to adapt to acute pressure. In one instance, it may have triggered a latent mania buried beneath a simply shy and undeveloped personality.

Over thirty-five years later during his murder trial, Kaczynski's lawyers attributed some of his emotional instability and dislike of mind control techniques to his participation in this study. His legal team attempted to enter an insanity defense to save Kaczynski's life, but Kaczynski rejected this plea. A court-appointed psychiatrist diagnosed him as suffering from paranoid schizophrenia but declared him competent to stand trial.

After graduating from Harvard at the age of 20 in 1962, Kaczynski continued his studies at the University of Michigan. At Michigan, he taught classes and worked on his widely lauded dissertation. Five years later he earned his doctoral degree.

Kaczynski was hired as an assistant professor of mathematics at the University of California at Berkeley for the 1967-68 and 1968-69 school years. The general catalog for the 1968-69 academic year shows Kaczynski was scheduled to teach four courses: Number Systems, Introduction to the Theory of Sets, General Topology and Function Spaces. He lived in a compact Regent Street apartment, remote from nearby campus vehicular and pedestrian traffic. Typified by colleagues as being pathologically shy, Kaczynski struggled at Berkeley. His abilities as a lecturer and his poor communications with students made his tenure impossible. His loner persona doubtlessly conflicted with the student protest mentality and activism of the era.

At Berkeley it was theorized that he developed a disdain for technology and many of the trappings of modern life. During his tenure, he was the author of six professional papers published between 1965 and 1969. He voluntarily and abruptly resigned from the university following the

1969 academic year and spent the next few years drifting from city to city. Was this defiant act the genesis of his degenerative personality?

In 1971 Kaczynski and his brother David purchased a plot of land near Lincoln, Montana and it was there that he would spend most of the ensuing 24 years. In a remote 10x12' cabin without electricity or running water, he lived as a recluse while learning survival skills in an attempt to become self-sufficient.

The intensity of his estrangement from society resulted in fatal consequences. From 1978 to 1995, Kaczynski sent 16 bombs to targets including universities and airlines, killing three people and injuring 23. How and why he selected his victims was never adequately publicly explained during his trial. Several of the injuries were unfortunate individuals who were responsible for opening incoming mail.

It is problematical to understand ideological homicide. How does one empathize with an individual who would randomly wound or kill without certainty of their intended victim? Surely he understood that each unique killing spawned numerous subsequent victims? Kaczynski's rational appeared the most pathological and senseless of motives; understood only by himself.

Kaczynski's unveiling and capture began when he anonymously mailed a letter to The *New York Times* on April 24, 1995. He promised to cease his killing spree if *The Times* or *Washington Post* published his now infamous *Unabomber Manifesto* (Industrial Society and Its Future). Apparently even recluses can succumb to the seduction of public exposure of their ideas.

The Times published his 35,000-word text that stressed the erosion of human freedom necessitated by modern technology. His brother David recognized many elements of the writing and forwarded his name to federal investigators. The tip led investigators to the Montana cabin where Ted Kaczynski was arrested on April 3, 1996.

The cabin featured a compacted trove of incriminating evidence linking Kaczynski to the attacks including journal entries, bomb diagrams and parts and handwritten drafts of his manifesto. Would his assaults realistically have ended with the publication of his *Manifesto*? No evidence was ever discovered to indicate either way except Kaczynski's promise.

Kaczynski was arraigned in California and New Jersey, the locations of his three fatal bombings. The victims included Hugh Scrutton, Thomas Mosser and Gilbert Murray. On January 22, 1998, he pleaded guilty to the charges against him in exchange for a sentence of life in prison without the possibility of parole. The sentence isolated Kaczynski even further from society and an explanation towards his precise motives.

Did he truly envision his *Manifesto* would alter the direction of civilization? It is not difficult to concur with his premise that society has restricted personal privacy and freedom with today's technology. It is a disturbing phenomenon that individuals may so freely discard rights, which required generations and centuries to earn.

Yet isolated homicides such as Kaczynski's have not impacted change in the slightest. His *Unabomber Manifesto* has not cracked the mandated reading lists of any recognized academic institution including his own. Were his observations, due to his mathematical genius more relevant than anyone else's?

Contemporary society has the capacity to estrange all social classes. Individuals are required to assimilate to the frenetic pace or risk being marginalized and alienated from the future. At some juncture, each individual may ultimately have to determine their jumping off point from the pace.

But at least for now, that option is freely given by choice.

Ted Kaczynski *Unabomber* Residence:
2628A Regent Street, Berkeley

The USS Hornet: Death On Board

The USS Hornet CV-12 currently docked in Alameda is the eighth battleship incarnation of the *Hornet* name. The initial was commissioned in 1775 and employed against the British in the Revolutionary War. The seventh was renowned for launching the *Doolittle Raid* against mainland Japan during World War II and fighting in the *Battle of Midway*. The ship was sunk at the *Battle of Santa Cruz*.

The eighth USS Hornet was commissioned in 1943 and became one of the most decorated Naval ships during both World War II and the Vietnam War. As a final service accolade, the vessel recovered astronauts from both the Apollo 11 and 12 missions

Aside from the fury of wartime battle, battleship life is extremely hazardous. Violent storms and gusts, snapped flight arrest cables, spinning propellers and deck explosions have contributed to an elevated level of onboard casualties. During 27 years of active service, more than 300 soldiers lost their lives aboard the ship. The majority were the result of combat casualties and shipboard hazards. Another contingent was attributable to suicides.

The USS Hornet has the unsavory distinction of suffering more suicides than any other ship in Naval history. Reports of haunting and paranormal activity have plagued the ship from the outset.

Anchored off Alameda Point's Pier 3, the decommissioned USS Hornet offers public access and tours of the ship. Odd phenomena have not entirely subsided.

In April 2007, volunteer Edward Vela III hung himself in

the engine room below decks. Vela's bizarre death seemed unexplainable to his peers, friends and acquaintances.

Volunteers freely offer their time and talent to keep the carrier afloat. Their commitment ranges from acting as docents to painting and helping restore mechanical parts on the boat. On such a vessel with its strange and tortured history, a curse appears to remain even in retirement

USS Hornet:
707 West Hornet Avenue, Pier 3, Alameda

Wagon Wheel Gambling Hall: The Cesspool That Was El Cerrito

Today's diminutive Fraternal Order of the Eagles Hall appears significantly distinct from its former identity as the Wagon Wheel Gambling Hall between 1935 into 1951. El Cerrito was considered an East Bay bedroom community but notoriously earned a reputation as a cesspool for gambling, dog racing, prostitution and vice. The dog-racing track opened in 1932 and operated adjacent to the Rancho San Pablo nightclub and casino. Ironically the nightclub was housed in the historic Castro Adobe constructed over one hundred years earlier by Spanish settle Don Victor Castro.

Future Nevada based *Mustang Ranch* proprietor Joe Conforte recounted in his memoirs his stint as a taxi driver during the 1950s shepherding *action seeking* clients to the vice options and delights that surrounded the El Cerrito racetrack.

The dog-racing track was demolished in 1948 to enable a drive-in movie theatre. The Castro house would be destroyed by fire in April 1956. Today's El Cerrito Plaza shopping center was constructed in 1958 atop the ashes and theatre demolition. The former Wagon Wheel Hall is one of the few reminders of an unrecognizable past.

**Wagon Wheel Gambling Hall:
3223 Carlson Boulevard, El Cerrito**

MARIN COUNTY

Artie and Jim Mitchell: Contemporary Cain and Abel

The ancient biblical Genesis account of Cain slaying his younger brother Abel appears remote and removed from contemporary culture. A morality tale, it often remains shelved and dust encrusted next to Shakespeare's historical tragedies. Most ancient and modern commentators assumed that Cain's motives were jealousy and anger triggered by his insufficient sacrifice to God, in comparison with his brother's.

Cain's often-repeated defense when asked the location of his dead brother was, *Am I My Brother's Keeper?* The expression simulates comparisons amidst the interweaving fate of brothers Jim and Artie Mitchell. Theirs is a classical murder story lacking heroes and conclusive explanations. Their narrative answers vanished with the victim's immediate death and the protagonist's demise a decade later. Yet the evil root was not fully severed by a single tragic act. Murder would resurface twenty years later by the actions of the perpetrator's male offspring.

The crime location city of Corte Madera is an intimate Marin Country suburb of 9,000+ where little of significance purposely occurs. Residents gravitate towards upscale conclaves like Corte Madera to escape the unpleasant realities of urban crime. Promoting minimal novelty except an occasional restaurant opening is sufficient. Stability and a sense of security are larger priorities and appreciating real estate values.

Within the San Francisco Bay area, suburban fortresses of protection are diminishing. Criminal activity has encroached beyond traditional civic boundaries. Random chaos sometimes infiltrates from the outside but more increasingly from within.

The street of Artie Mitchell's homicide resembles innumerable American neighborhoods. The houses lack extravagance despite their equity value and indistinguishable facades appear absent of menace. Early morning weekday commutes vacate the neighborhood. Weeknight and weekend foot and vehicle traffic are negligible.

On one arbitrary evening during the winter of 1991, the veil of invincibility was lifted.

Artie Mitchell lived in a community like Corte Madera to escape his own contentious workplace, located on the periphery of the outer Tenderloin district of San Francisco. The Tenderloin has been forever seemingly a refuge of the homeless, mentally ill and marginalized outcasts of society. Artie Mitchell was the co-proprietor of the O'Farrell Theatre, then one of the most influential pornography film production and sex club companies nationally.

The O'Farrell Theatre was founded in 1969 by Artie's older brother Jim and became the epicenter of San Francisco debate over public obscenity enforcement regulations. Jim, the elder by three years, mentored Artie into the enterprise assuming the role of his Brother's Keeper. The brother's were raised in Antioch and considered close. Their father made his livelihood as a professional gambler. Their mother was a homemaker. There were never published disclosures indicating any form of abnormal dysfunction within their family unit.

Jim inherited his father's speculative intuition. He attended San Francisco State University focusing on film courses. His supplementary work in pornography cinema convinced him this medium offered significant unrealized financial potential. His instinct proved correct. The brothers collectively pioneered profitable, efficiently budgeted films even if an actual plotline proved as absent as the clothing on participating actors and actresses.

The enterprise sprouted into eleven operating theatres by 1974 and a prominent rostrum of public supporters and clientele. Their biggest mainstream audience success became the 1971 production of *Behind the Green Door* grossing reportedly in excess of $25 million based on a modest $60,000 production budget.

The brothers remained cohesive publicly but personality differences, Artie's reported drug abuse and rumors of financial mismanagement created extreme dissension internally. Jim assumed responsibility for cleaning up the mess and determined a direct confrontation with Artie was the best way.

The tragedy following his approach created speculation towards his genuine motivations. Were they based on concern towards his brother's erratic behavior or premeditated murder designed to end hemorrhaging cashflow? Only Jim Mitchell could account for his actions. Disclosure was not forthcoming at his public murder trial.

Jim Mitchell drove to Artie's tranquil Corte Madera residence on the evening of February 27, 1991. He arrived unannounced, hushed and armed at the front entrance parking lot. The sole potential witness was Artie's live-in girlfriend Julie Bajo.

Hearing outside rustlings while lounging in bed, Artie approached his front door cautiously armed with a pistol. Bajo barricaded herself in a bedroom closet mute and terrified. She claimed to have heard neither conversation nor warning before the shooting. Did Artie Mitchell cautiously walk into an impending ambush?

Jim pumped eight rounds from a .22 rifle into his brother killing him instantly in the driveway. Artie's pistol was not discharged. Mitchell was apprehended 100 yards down the block from Artie's home presumably returning to his car. He had stuffed the fired rifle into a pants leg and also carried an unfired pistol in a holster. In a community where little of significant happens, the police response was immediate.

At Jim Mitchell's trial, prosecutors presented a computer-generated video recreation of the killing. It was the first time this technology was employed in a murder trial. Mitchell testified his actions were prompted by an earlier conversation with Artie, whose tone was angry and threatening when confronted about his substance abuse. Mitchell further claimed he used the rifle as a bluff tactic for intimidation purposes, but as Artie elevated his pistol towards him, he felt compelled to retaliate in self-defense. His testimony included a memory loss of events transpiring after firing the first round and being apprehended.

The jury found Mitchell not guilty of murder but guilty of voluntary manslaughter. He was also convicted of unlawfully discharging a firearm and brandishing a firearm to a police officer. Several notable San Francisco political luminaries and law enforcement officials spoke on his behalf-requesting leniency during the sentencing phase.

In 1992, Jim was sentenced to three years for manslaughter and an additional three for the use of the firearm. Five and a half years later, he was released from San Quentin Prison followed up by three years on parole. He controversially founded an *Artie Fund* to support a local drug treatment center. Artie's children denounced his effort finding it outrageous that their father's killer would have the audacity to honor him after the act. Ten years later Jim died of a heart attack and was buried in his native Antioch adjacent to Artie.

This apparent closure did not cease the family curse. In 2009, Jim's son James savagely murdered Danielle Keller, the mother of his two-year-old daughter, in spite of an outstanding restraining order against him. The site of the killing was in suburban Novato, located fifteen miles from Corte Madera. In 2011, James was convicted and sentenced from thirty-five years to life for first-degree murder, kidnapping and assorted domestic violence charges. He is currently interned at the RJ Donovan

The enduring legacy of Cain's act to his brother Abel reminds us our innate nature and actions have not altered profoundly throughout the centuries. Our protective suburban citadels simply prove inadequate against the fatal occurrences of primal behavior.

Artie Mitchell's Murder Site:
23 Mohawk Avenue, Corte Madera

O'Farrell Theatre (Owned by the Mitchell Brothers):
895 O'Farrell Street, San Francisco

Blue Rock Inn: From Resort to Scandal to Cornerstone

Opened in 1897 as an 80-room hotel near the North Pacific Railroad line, the Blue Rock Inn originally accommodated weekend San Francisco visitors seeking to hunt, fish or simply escape the shrouded fog. C. W. Wright of Oakland purchased the majority of present day Larkspur operating the hotel along with a saltwater bathhouse across the street.

The hotel took advantage of the free-flowing slough that emptied into the San Francisco Bay. The ground floor of the property was constructed with blue basalt rock from a nearby quarry providing the hotel's namesake.

Larkspur during the early twentieth century was a haven for vice featuring illegal dog races, prizefights and gambling. Prohibition introduced bootlegging and prostitution.

Times have radically changed in the affluent community. As Marin County gentrified during post World War II, the Inn transformed into a distinctively fine dining establishment. The current establishment, the Left Bank Brasserie extends its reformed reputation and has become a cornerstone in Larkspur's dining options.

Blue Rock Inn:
507 Magnolia Avenue, Larkspur

Litchfield's: A Solitary Neon Sign Conveying a Forgotten Legacy

San Rafael will never be mistaken for Las Vegas, but between the 1940s and 70s, Litchfield's Bermuda Palms was self-promoted as *California's Las Vegas*. Millionaire construction mogul Irving *Whitey* Litchfield built his resort in the late 1940s with a luxury swimming pool, color television, nightly dancing and marginally priced rooms. His Flamingo ballroom attracted some of the music industry's top acts including Duke Ellington, the Grateful Dead, Janis Joplin, Chuck Berry and even Pink Floyd. Highly touted strippers such as Lili St. Cyr attracted audiences drawn primarily from Marin County and San Francisco.

Celebrities and particularly famed boxers (Litchfield had been an amateur boxer) frequented regularly. In 1954, Humphrey Bogart, John Wayne, Lauren Bacall and Robert Mitchum resided there while filming *Blood Alley* nearby at China Camp.

Litchfield created the property as a *hobby* and he extensively promoted the location. He installed an expansive neon sign conspicuously visible to passing motorists along Highway 101.

San Rafael's Canal neighborhood declined significantly during the 1970s and Litchfield's motel on East Francisco Boulevard remained on the frontline. As drugs, prostitution and violence proliferated, the neighborhood grew dangerous. Police vice raids frequently targeted the Bermuda Palms.

Litchfield perpetually claimed that he lacked support from the San Rafael police and city government. He fought during the declining years to keep the property open and used his marquee as a propaganda message board. In 1988, he closed down the motel and removed his remaining tenants except those placed there by the country welfare department.

The property had long ceased to be a drawing magnet and was instead a pariah to avoid. Litchfield died in 1995 and a horse-drawn carriage transported his coffin to St. Paul's Episcopal Church where more than 200 mourners honored him. His memorial service program was printed on a racing form.

The Bermuda Palms has been transformed into a homogenous Motel 6 with no remembrances of its former grandeur. The Litchfield sign defiantly remains upon the roof of a converted furniture store.

The ranks of extravagant promoters and nonconformists such as Whitey Litchfield are thinning. San Rafael remains a hybrid of suburban conformity laced by a confirmed homeless contingent. Most viewers of the Litchfield sign are inclined to speculate that it once belonged to a defunct grocery store.

California's Las Vegas seems as hallucinatory as the drugs once proliferating for sale on the neighborhood's street corners.

Litchfield's Bermuda Palms:
745 Francisco Blvd East, San Rafael

The Marin County Courthouse Shootout: Thirty Minutes That Forever Altered Courtroom Security Procedures

The final commission of architect Frank Lloyd Wright was the design of the majestic Marin Civic Center and Administration Building in San Rafael. Groundbreaking for the complex was initiated in 1960 after Wright's death and completed in 1962. The Hall of Justice section was begun in 1966 and completed in 1969.

On August 7, 1970, only one year after completion of the Hall of Justice, the Marin County Superior Court was the scene of an attempted jailbreak and hostage trade led by 17-year-old Jonathan Jackson, the brother of Black Panther militant George Jackson.

Jackson's motivation was an attempt to negotiate the freedom of the *Soledad Brothers* by kidnapping Superior Court Judge Harold Haley and other courtroom hostages. *The Soledad Brothers* consisted of George Jackson. Fleeta Drumgo, and John Clutchette, who were being held in San Quentin Prison awaiting trial for the murder of prison guard John Mills. Mills had been beaten and thrown from the third floor of Soledad's Y wing. George Jackson was a co-founder of the *Black Guerrilla Family* gang while incarcerated whose member, Tyrone Robinson (now Kambui Tyrone Robinson) would later murder Huey P. Newton.

The thirty-minute long ordeal began by a routine trial of defendant James D. McClain, a prisoner at San Quentin, who Haley allowed to represent himself. He had been charged with possession of a knife and stabbing a prison guard. As part of his defense four fellow prisoners from San Quentin were called to testify on his behalf. Ruchell

293

Magee was on the witness stand when Jonathan Jackson rose from the audience and disrupted the proceedings by raising a pistol towards the judicial stand.

In the chaos that followed, Jackson removed two additional guns from a satchel, which he had carried in. He distributed his pistol and the two guns to Magee, McClain and William Christmas, who had been in a holding cell waiting to be called to testify. He then produced a sawed-off shotgun hidden from within his raincoat. The kidnappers, after some debate, secured five hostages whom they bound with piano wire: Judge Haley, Deputy District Attorney Gary Thomas and jurors Maria Elena Graham, Doris Whitmer, and Joyce Rodoni.

Judge Haley was forced at gunpoint to call the courthouse bailiff with the intention of convincing the police to refrain from intervening. The sawed-off shotgun was held against Haley's neck as the four kidnappers and four other hostages then moved into the corridor of the courthouse inching their way towards the elevator.

The corridor was crowded with responding police but no action was taken against the kidnappers at that point.

The group entered the elevator demanding the freedom of the Soledad Brothers by 12:30 p.m. that day. The kidnappers then sheparded the hostages from the building into a rented Ford panel truck Jackson had left in the parking lot behind the courthouse.

Jackson's plan was ill conceived and doomed. Then California Governor Ronald Reagan would have never accommodated a hostage trade. Law enforcement personnel onsite had no intention of allowing the vehicle to leave the main driveway, the only exit, towards their destination of nearby Highway 101.

Police and San Quentin guards had set up a roadblock on both sides of the Hall of Justice driveway in anticipation of the group. According to eyewitnesses, law enforcement officers began to open fire on the van almost immediately after it had left the lobby pick-up point. A shootout resulted in which Jackson, McClain and Christmas were killed and Magee was seriously injured. Reports indicated that Thomas grabbed one of the kidnapper's guns and began firing at them from inside the van. Blood splattered everywhere from the resulting carnage.

Haley was slain by a discharge of the shotgun by Magee. Thomas was seriously wounded in his back, leaving him wheelchair-bound and Graham suffered a wound to her arm. Magee was shot in the chest and was taken to the hospital for emergency surgery.

The drama did not conclude with the August 7th butchery. A warrant was issued for the arrest of Angela Davis, a renowned communist activist and former professor in the University of California system. She had lived with and had a relationship with George Jackson prior to his incarceration. Davis was the registered owner of each of the employed guns including the sawed-off shotgun. Circumstantial evidence and eyewitnesses placed her in Jonathan Jackson's company just prior to the attempted kidnapping.

Davis became a glamorized cause celebre amongst anti-establishment causes during this era. Was she singled out for persecution by authorities or an active participant? She evaded capture for two months, hiding amongst her political connections before finally being arrested in New York City. She was charged as an accomplice to conspiracy, kidnapping, and homicide. She was tried in 1972 and found not guilty on each of the counts.

Ruchell Magee pled guilty to the charge of aggravated kidnapping for his part in the assault. He was sentenced in 1975 to life in prison and is currently serving his term at the California Men's Colony in San Luis Obispo.

George Jackson, who's hoped for release prompted the tragedy, was killed three days before he was to go on trial for prison guard Mill's murder. He was fatally shot in 1971 during a San Quentin riot attempting to escape. Ironically Drumgo and Clutchette, the remaining Soledad Brothers were acquitted of the murder.

Two unidentified men shot Fleeta Drumgo to death on November 27, 1979 on the streets of Oakland. He had been released from prison in 1976 after serving nine years for a Los Angeles burglary and was living with John Clutchette at the time. His killers were never caught. John Clutchette was released on parole in June 2018 after serving his sentence at the California State Prison Solano in Vacaville for a 1980 first-degree murder conviction. He was convicted of shooting Robert Bowles in the back of the head without warning or provocation over a drug-deal dispute.

In retrospect, many factors were conveniently ignored in assigning sole blame for Jonathan Jackson's actions. It is inconceivable that a seventeen-year-old man would have had the capacity or capability of orchestrating a suicidal hostage kidnapping. At seventeen, Jackson could not have legally rented a van or secured the necessary firearms without assistance.

Any potential associate conspirator(s) have never been

condemned to their due justice. Their hands remain stained by the shed blood of two honorable judicial figures and a teenager who simply wanted his older brother reunited with him. Jackson's motive was clear, misguided, but understandable. For those who evaded punishment by manipulating Jonathan Jackson to die in their place, their role is unconscionable.

The system of tight security prevalent in courtrooms today began with this incident in Marin County. Local courts were immediately wired with direct communication to the sheriff's department, and metal detectors were installed in all the courtrooms.

We take these precautions today for granted. One cannot fathom the vulnerability of a facility that could enable firearms to be effortless smuggled into a courtroom. This expectation of preventative security illuminates the level of eroded and vanished respect for our institutions of authority. Far worse, no one is even astonished.

Marin County Courthouse Shootout:
3501 Civic Center Drive, San Rafael

David Carpenter: The Devil Behind Bifocals and a Stutter

The remarkable longevity of convicted serial killer David Carpenter as he nears 90 is testament towards the merits or abuses of the appeal capabilities of convicts. Born in 1930, he is the oldest inmate at San Quentin and one of the oldest in the United States awaiting a death sentence that will doubtlessly be preceded by his own demise by natural causes.

The media labeled *Trailside Killer* was a notably shy, social introvert with a severe stutter. His personality and disability were coupled by a prototype serial killer history of violent crimes and sexual deviancy. His unremarkable, bespectacled and balding appearance separated him from the menacing attributes of assumed maniacal behavior. He spent more than 22 of his first 55 years in custody before his final incarceration.

His only conventional behavior appeared to be his first marriage at 25 that bore three children. His entrenched sexual perversion and disintegrating personality cracks were by then sufficiently evident but usually overlooked due to his nondescript physical features.

The formation behind the notorious predator and deviant were established early by reported animal torturing, physical abuse by his parents and an alcoholic father. At seventeen he was arrested for behavior that later became his defining compulsions. He spent three months at Napa State Hospital for molesting two of his cousins, one only three years old. The seeds towards complete unraveling continued in 1950 as he was arrested for raping a 17-year old girl but the charges were dropped. Throughout his life, he has maintained innocence for his actions. This pattern of

300

denial and disregard has never wavered even into his advanced age.

In 1960, the married Carpenter assaulted and nearly killed a woman he had befriended. She had rebuffed his clumsy seduction advances. Driving her into an isolated sector of San Francisco's Presidio Woods instead of her workplace, he struck her multiple times with a hammer. He fired upon a responding military patrol officer but missed. The officer wounded Carpenter with return fire and spared an initial murder victim as the woman survived.

He was arrested and sentenced to fourteen years of imprisonment. During his confinement, his wife divorced him. He learned valuable lessons about evading suspicion during his internment. He parroted for evaluating psychologists studied explanations rationalizing his erratic behavior. The ploy was successful as he served only nine years. He had learned to articulate what authorities and potential victims wished to hear, milking his stutter to maximum sympathetic effect. He also discovered that the best way to avoid returning to prison was to eliminate potential witnesses.

Released in 1969, he remarried quickly. Shortly afterwards, he sexually attacked two women in Santa Cruz County, stole a car and drove to the Sierra mountain region. In Calaveras County, he robbed two women, kidnapping one of them. He attempted to rape one woman that same year by striking her car and forcing her out. She resisted and was able to escape despite multiple stab wounds. He was arrested in Modesto in February 1970.

While awaiting trial for his crime spree, Carpenter attempted unsuccessfully to escape the Calaveras County jail. He was sentenced to seven years for kidnapping and robbery plus two for parole violation, He served the full sentence. All sex related offenses were dropped. Freed from the tracking designation of registered sex offender, his worse transgressions were to follow.

Carpenter typified the most dangerous sociopathic form of serial killer. He could superficially pass for a normal, articulate and productive citizen. He made the expected adaptation towards reform following his release from prison. He enrolled in a San Francisco based computer-printing course, graduating with a degree that enabled immediate employment. He became an instructor at an East Bay area agency affiliated with the school. He likewise became an avid hiker with designs on becoming a proficient stalker and camouflaged predator.

His multiple guises proved useful for the killing sequence to follow. Between 1979-1981 months after his release, he raped and murdered ten confirmed victims and two suspected. Based on his pathological cunning and impulses, the fatality totals could be easily understated. During that same period, several remote terrain killers roamed the Marin, Sonoma and Santa Cruz mountain regions.

His tactics were varied, efficient and gruesome. Each victim was alone on isolated stretches of the publicly hiked trails.

All of the victims were surprised from behind or blind vantage points. It is assumed the killer deliberately stalked and patiently awaited his prey. Some were shot, generally to the head or stabbed repeatedly and viciously. One victim was strangled with picture framing wire. Most of the women were attractive, slight and in their 20s. Each was overwhelmed by his superior strength. The victims that he struck were aggressively beaten and often raped. A FBI profiler surmised that an execution-style killing employed on a few of the victims, while on their knees, may have been a forced subservience gesture by Carpenter to assert his perceived male superiority.

A sadist such as Carpenter doubtlessly endured tremendous trauma and ridicule due to his lifelong stutter. His stutter also generated significant empathy, which he manipulated. It was suggested that this sympathy disarmed many of his potential victims before his lethal attacks. Some of his survivors indicated his pronounced stutter was absent during his attacks.

His appearance, which made him invisible as a person, distinguished him as a rapist. A middle-aged balding male wearing glass could be very identifiable in a police line-up. Eliminating his victims became imperative.

The list of confirmed Mt. Tamalpais trail victims included Edda Kane (1979), Barbara Schwartz (1980), Anna Mejivas (1980) and Anne Anderson (1990). Shawna May and Diane O'Connell, strangers to each other, were murdered at the Point Reyes National Seashore Park. They were discovered lain adjacently face down in a shallow ditch. It was speculated that one of victims had appeared inconveniently while Carpenter was violating the other. Both were killed at approximately the same time on November 28, 1980.

On the following day, their bodies and two other buried victims, Cynthia Moreland and Richard Towers, were discovered a half-mile away. Morehead and Towers had been slain the month previously. Investigators surmised that although the locations were different, the killings were committed only days apart from Anne Anderson's.

A concealed eyewitness viewed the stabbing of Barbara

Schwartz and provided police with a detailed description of the assailant. Her physical profile proved erroneous and the inaccuracies hindered the police initially. Other hikers fortunately spotted Carpenter following some of the murders ultimately enabling police to compose a more accurate composite profile sketch of the killer.

Like the more renowned Zodiac serial killer, Carpenter only attacked males when they accompanied their female partners. Their appearance may have come as a problematical surprise. Their immediate elimination became paramount to avoid a more equally matched struggle or detection. Stealth and surprise were elemental to his attacking strategy. As with the Zodiac, cowardice towards a male presence threatened his perceived sense of gender dominance.

Expanding his network of killing sites, he killed Ellen Hansen in 1981 at a park near Santa Cruz, but made a crucial error. Her boyfriend, Steve Haertle survived the attack despite being shot four times, twice through his neck. Haertle furnished police with a crucial description of the assailant and his distinctive escape vehicle, a red Fiat.

Carpenter had evaded capture for two years despite widespread public and law enforcement attention. In May of 1981, he kidnapped and killed a co-worker, Heather Scaggs. He had stupidity and in all probability arrogantly killed a victim directly traceable to him.

Scaggs had informed her boyfriend about an impending visit to Carpenter's house because he was going to assist her in purchasing a used car. When investigating officers questioned Carpenter regarding Scagg's visit and subsequent disappearance at his San Francisco residence, they observed his resemblance to the Trailside killer's composite sketch. His red Fiat further linked him to Ellen Hansen's killing. The survivor of the attack, Steve Haertle identified Carpenter in a police line-up.

The focus of examination abruptly honed in on him. His multiple felonies and incarcerations had previously eluded scrutiny due to a variety of bureaucratic errors. Once examined, his profile made him an obvious candidate. The subsequent investigation and apprehension of Carpenter followed swiftly.

Upon the discovery of Heather Scagg's body in Big Basin State Park in the Santa Cruz Mountains, Carpenter was arrested for her homicide. An escalating case of evidence was building against him. A selling party for one of his primary .45 caliber pistols, used in several of the killings, came forward. The gun was never recovered. A second weapon however, used in the final two killings was discovered by investigators and submitted into evidence by the prosecution.

David Carpenter was convicted for the first-degree murders of Hansen and Skaggs in July of 1984 and separately convicted of five Marin murders later in the year. He was sentenced to death on November 16, 1984. He was not charged in some of the Marin trails cases and two suspected killings. These two included Anna K. Menjivar, a 17-year old high school student killed in 1981 at Castle Rock State Park in the Santa Cruz Mountains. She worked at a bank that Carpenter habitually patronized. In 2009, DNA evidence linked him to the 1979 violent stabbing death of Mary Frances Bennett who had been jogging near the Palace of the Legion of Honor when attacked.

Over three and a half decades have passed in confinement. Carpenter is apparently respected and well regarded by his peers (not surprising) and compliant to prison authority. In a 2013 published interview with convict/journalist Boston Woodard, he maintained his steadfast innocence of all convicted charges and boasted about his good health, despite nearing ninety. Carpenter indicated that the majority of his time was spent with written correspondence, legal appeal documentation and regular attendance at Catholic worship services. His continued appeals and legal efforts have delayed his ultimate execution.

A profound absence of remorse towards his crimes and murder victims remains entrenched within his crippled and corrupt soul. Instead, his complaints about zealous law enforcement persecution become hollow and as rote as his earlier psychological rationalizations. He is an individual who has learned nothing constructive or introspectively from his life of debauchery.

His life remains conclusive proof that habitual violent criminals are beyond redemption even with an unthreatening demeanor and appearance. Despite certain similarities with the Zodiac killings, he was dismissed long ago as a suspect due to his incarceration at the identical times of the murders.

His legal appeals and requests for new trials have been routinely and systematically denied. Each attempt strains an overloaded legal system and lengthens his condemned life.

Since 1978, the average time served on death row has been 17 1/2 years and 49 is the average age at execution. There are currently approximately 741 prisoners on death row in California, by far the most populous state compared to Texas and Florida, active states for executions. During that same period, over 60 condemned prisoners have died from natural causes, 22 have committed suicide and only 13, predominately white males, have been executed. The last execution was in 2006.

It is unlikely Carpenter will share their fate. The travesty that has defined his delay is an affront society's notion of expedient justice.

What seems difficult to determine is which option is more repulsive, his deeds or his denials.

**Trailhead Killer David Carpenter's Residence:
38 Sussex Street, San Francisco**

Mount Tamalpais Trailhead:
3801 Panoramic Highway, Mill Valley

The Marin County Barbeque Murders

This twisted narrative appears on the surface like a classic film noir story of deception and manipulated murder. A femme fatale teenager convinces her obsessed older boyfriend to murder her abusive parents. The plot deepens when a ferociously struck hammer blow to the head kills the mother. Who is the responsible party?

The girl's father is consequently shot to death upon returning home unexpectedly following the killing. Was his death the result of falsely assuming the boyfriend's guilt for his wife's death?

Nothing appears entirely clear in evaluating this story decades later.

What is known is that on June 21, 1975, Naomi and Jim Olive were murdered inside their Terra Linda residence. Their bodies were then transported by the killers to a barbeque pit at the nearby China Camp recreational park. They were doused with gasoline and burned. The perpetrators abandoned the park briefly while the bodies were smoldering. During their absence, the reduced corpses were discovered by a fireman and mistaken for a deer carcass. The responsible parties returned later to dispose of the remains.

The victims, Jim and Naomi Olive had settled in Marin County during the early 1970s after he lost his marketing job with an oil company in Guayaquil, Ecuador. Upon his return, he began a small business consultancy. During the couple's residence overseas, they adopted Marlene. She had spent her childhood and early teen years in Ecuador.

The return transition into a Northern California way of life proved challenging. The family was splintering. Marlene fought constantly with her mother. Her father's priorities were devoted towards establishing his business enterprise and their relationship became distant.

Marlene felt alienated amidst the more permissive local teenage culture. Her sheltered existence in Ecuador had not prepared her for such an extreme clash of values. She gravitated towards other outsiders, immersed in drugs, alternative music, witchcraft and even reportedly prostitution.

One of her drug suppliers, 19-years-old Charles *Chuck* Riley found Marlene an ideal solution for his own demons and ingrained sense of inadequacy. Riley weighed in excess of 300 pounds. His childhood obesity kept him socially solitary and lonely. He was anxious to reward any attention that Marlene paid him. He supplied her with free drugs, transportation and gifts. She was his first girlfriend. Eventually, despite her revulsion regarding his weight, they became lovers.

Marlene controlled their fragile relationship, breaking up with him on multiple occasions to reaffirm her dominance. One of her ongoing confided obsessions included murdering her adoptive parents. She sensed that she had recruited the proper foil based on his desire to please her and fascination with guns.

Months prior to the murder, the pair went on an extended shoplifting spree. They were caught in the act and arrested for grand larceny. Their arraignment provoked Marlene's parents to permanently forbid her from spending time with Riley.

Riley was arrested a second time in May 1975 for

possession of marijuana and a sawed-off shotgun. His life was unraveling and the sole intact strand appeared to be the volatile Marlene. Now he was losing her.

Her parent's prohibition prompted more disagreements. Riley blamed Marlene on instigating the murder. She protested her innocence claiming the killing was carried out by Riley exclusively. Two versions of the unfolding drama were introduced during their trial.

Most of the facts were drawn from Riley's original confession. According to his version, Marlene summoned him by phone following a heated argument with her mother. The dispute likely concerned their relationship.

Realizing he might permanently lose access to her, he agreed to finally carry out Marlene's ongoing request to kill her parents. Marlene left a door unlocked while her mother slept. She had arranged to meet with her father away from the house for an undisclosed reason. Riley confessed to having ingested LSD before his arrival. He entered the Olive residence with a loaded .22 caliber revolver. Upon viewing the sleeping Naomi Olive, he confessed to having struck her many times with a hammer, stabbed her and finally suffocated her. Such a killing frenzy seemed odd directed towards someone he was scarcely acquainted with.

Before Riley had vacated the house, James Olive returned. Viewing the carnage, he grabbed a knife and approached Riley with the intention to kill him. Riley instinctively responded by shooting him fatally four times with his revolver.

This account seemed plausible to a jury. His detachment from the events seemed explainable based on Riley and Olive's behavior afterwards.

The doomed couple, with help from friends, attempted to sanitize the killing location. The pair remained in the house for several days. They attended a rock concert, shopped and ate out, covering their expenses with her parent's cash, checks and credit cards. Remorse for their act was nonexistent.

As inquiries about Jim Olive's whereabouts started, Marlene began fabricating excuses for her parent's disappearance. A police visit to the house confirmed something was amiss and inconsistent with her story. The murder room was the sole orderly area in a household of complete disarray.

Acting on a tip, the police discovered the disposal barbeque pit. They determined that it had contained fragments of burnt human remains. Although DNA evidence had not yet been fully developed, they felt confident enough over the couple's guilt to arrest and charge both with the murders.

A seemingly straightforward killing with motive took multiple swerves during the trial. Finally cognizant regarding the severity of the charges against him and freed from the burden of protecting Marlene, Chuck Riley began to alter his portrayal of events.

Under hypnosis, Riley recanted parts of his initial confession. He indicated that upon entering the Olive household, he had found Naomi Olive bleeding profusely from head wounds and near death. He speculated that Marlene had struck her mother in the skull earlier with a hammer. The employed tool had been initially used to repair one of Marlene's loosened platform soles. He claimed that he suffocated Naomi simply to end her misery and shot James out of fear and self-defense before being lethally attacked. He stressed that his original confession was given solely to protect Marlene from guilt.

The ferocity of the hammer blows seemed to corroborate his revised version, but was viewed with suspicion. Marlene did appear a more credible suspect in her mother's death.

The jury concluded Riley's amended confession lacked credibility and pronounced him solely guilty of the double murder and sentenced to the death penalty. In 1976, when capital punishment was temporarily rescinded in California, his term was changed to life imprisonment with the possibility of parole.

Based on her juvenile status, Marlene Olive was convicted of a Section 602 charge. This nebulous violation covered crimes committed by a minor ranging from petty theft up to murder. She served four years at the California Youth Authority Center in Ventura and was released.

The futures of Chuck Riley and Marlene Olive veered into distinctly diverse directions upon his incarceration. She would visit him only a single time in prison during 1981.

While at San Quentin, Riley lost his girth and earned the equivalent of a college degree. He applied for parole a dozen times and was routinely denied. Finally in 2015, the California parole board ruled him fit for release. Governor Jerry Brown overturned their ruling. In an odd twist of fate, Riley appealed Brown's decision and won. He was released from prison in December 2015.

Marlene Olive's reformation took an immediate nosedive during her initial correctional stay. Weeks before her parole date, she escaped and moved to New York City where she worked as a prostitute. She was apprehended and returned to complete her California term.

Upon her official release, she relocated to Los Angeles and began a forgery, identity theft and drug ring. She was arrested and changed her name on multiple occasions before relocating to Bakersfield to resume her illegal activities. She was once again caught passing fictitious checks and sentenced to seven years in prison. She has since been paroled but the question persists, under which alias?

Chuck Riley and Marlene Olive's cautionary example exemplifies two aimless lives that lacked direction. Riley may one day contribute something positive to society. Olive has made her intention abundantly clear that she has no desire to.

Olive Couple Murder:
353 Hibiscus Way, Terra Linda

China Camp Recreational Park:
100 China Camp Village Road, San Rafael

Robin Williams: The Self-Destructive Tears of a Harlequin

The funniest man in the room may have ultimately been the saddest and most desperate for attention. Robin Williams introduced his stream of consciousness banter of humor that captivated stage and screen audiences globally. Unfortunately, a darker internal depression permeated profoundly.

The distinctive lines between pathos and laughter were etched on Williams' face as he accomplished through his performances something few comics ever attain. He could touch audiences emotionally with his tenderness and vulnerability. His serious acting performances sliced through the veil of the clown masked by rubbery facial expressions. He understood emotional trauma because he silently co-existed with conflictive emotions the majority of his life.

He was introduced to mass audiences through television, but his signature improvisational style was honed through comedy venues in San Francisco and Los Angeles in the mid-1970s. Along with television, he achieved international acclaim through a tapestry of feature films and animated voice over characters.

He was nominated four times for Academy Awards, winning once as Best Supporting Actor. Yet such accolades seem insufficient for a talent that merited its own unique category.

Williams was raised in comfortable affluence in Illinois and Michigan. At sixteen, the family moved to Tiburon in Marin County when his father decided upon an early retirement. He attended high school and later community college in nearby Larkspur. His high school classmates voted him in 1969 as *Funniest* and *Least Likely to Succeed*. He briefly studied political science his freshman year at the Claremont Men's College before finding a more comfortable niche for three years at the Juilliard School of Arts in New York. His peers included Christopher Reeve, William Hurt, Mandy Patinkin and Franklyn Seales. Each later distinguished themselves professionally.

His stand-up comic performances became legendary. The accompanying stress involved from a touring lifestyle involving partying, drinking and drugs proved brutal towards his establishing personality equilibrium. His creative process and delivery bordered on manic. Many spectators and critics felt his frenetic and intense mental state often bordered on a complete meltdown.

Their observations were valid.

William's personal life was predictably chaotic and messy. He was married three times and had three children. He was reputed to be a caring and exemplary father. He relished private moments with his family and strived to protect them from the intrusions of celebrity.

Williams battled alcohol addiction and substance abuse for most of this adult life. He spent the evening partying with friend John Belushi the day before he overdosed in 1982. He employed cycling, exercise and therapy to treat his severe depression and anxiety issues. In 2009, he was hospitalized due to heart problems that required surgery to replace his aortic valve.

The circumstances leading up to his eventual suicide in 2014 were attributed to severe depression, early stage Parkinson's disease and diffuse Lewy body dementia.

Whatever the precise influence, Robin Williams was conscious that he was a very unhappy individual. His own perceived prognosis concluded that his continued physical and mental deterioration was inevitable.

His death occurred at his seaside house in Tiburon, the same city where his assent into performance began.

On Sunday, August 10, 2014, his wife last saw him alive at 10:30 p.m. when she retired for bed. The couple slept in separate rooms. He seated himself fully clothed with a belt secured around his neck. The other end of the belt wedged between the clothes closet door and doorframe. His right shoulder was touching the door and his body was perpendicular to the door and slightly suspended.

The following morning at 11:45 a.m. when he failed to answer knocks upon his bedroom door, he was discovered deceased by his personal assistant. The coroner officially declared his death *due to asphyxia from hanging*.

His passing was mourned internationally. Few could (and still) understand how someone who conveyed such joy and stimulated so much laughter in others could feel so miserable and empty internally.

There are no answers that will ever prove satisfactory.

Robin Williams Suicide Site:
95 Saint Thomas Way, Tiburon

Sally Stanford's Gilded Age

Her surname was lifted from the Palo Alto based university. The most embellished narratives about her life are probably true. Sally Stanford was a feline of many lives and her varied exploits were worthy of literature and film. In her autobiography *Lady of the House* she confessed that she adopted the name *Stanford* after reading about the university winning a football game. It would not be her sole pseudonym in a life rife with audacious self-promotion.

What appears factually known about her is that she was born in 1903 as Mabel Janice Busby in Oregon and originally arrived into San Francisco in 1924.

She was Madame at a famed brothel on 1144 Pine Street designed by architect Stanford White. *San Francisco Chronicle* columnist Herb Caen wrote *that the United Nations was founded at Sally Stanford's whorehouse*. He based his claim due to the number of 1945 founding member delegates that were Stanford's clients. He elaborated that many of the UN's negotiating sessions took place in the brothel's living room. Perhaps exaggeration, perhaps truth...an amusing tale nonetheless. The building was demolished in 1961 to construct homogenous condominiums.

Stanford's two additional San Francisco bordellos remain on the fringes of the downtown's Tenderloin. Despite their location, they radiate stately classical taste.

In 1950, she transferred her residence and livelihood to coastal Sausalito where she reopened the former *Walhalla* restaurant and renamed it the *Valhalla Inn*. The change in venue expanded her personal celebrity. The restaurant became a popular gathering place for locals, celebrities and straying San Franciscans. The red light stationed in the rear of the establishment served either as a public tease or beacon of invitation for dessert.

During her residence in Sausalito, she became active locally and ran for the city council six times. She finally won in 1972 and was elected mayor the same year by her peers. As an honorarium for her perseverance, she was named the city's *Vice Mayor For Life*.

It is fruitless to separate fact from myth concerning a gargantuan personality like Sally Stanford. One reported anecdote that best illuminates her audacity was her 1967 surprise attendance at the men's luncheon during the California Jaycees Annual Convention. With feathered boa draping an ornate, floor-length gown, she personally greeted members of the head table with a familiar hug and kiss on their cheek. The dignitaries included Senator Ted Kennedy, San Francisco Mayor Joseph Alioto, attorney Melvin Belli and the newly elected president of the Jaycees. She then took the podium and informed the audience that each had been or were current clients.

No one publicly disputed the accuracy of her claim.

She passed away in February 1982 and her Valhalla Inn building staggered through a succession of tenants, permanently closing in 2009. Several subsequent projects including a 20-room boutique hotel were proposed and scrapped until the city council's 2018 acceptance of a dual unit condominium project. Construction is underway with an anticipated late 2019-2020 completion date. A rectangular section of the original building's wood siding crowns the new construction's roof.

Perhaps it is an appropriate memento of the uncrowned but omnipresent Queen Sally of Sausalito.

Sally Sanford's Brothel:
610 Leavenworth Street, San Francisco

Sally Sanford's Brothel:
695 O'Farrell Street, San Francisco

**Sally Sanford's Valhalla Inn:
201 Bridgeway, Sausalito**

PENINSULA

The Kidnapping of Brooke Hart and Resulting Mob Justice

Localized public outrage and righteous indignation appear in diminishing exhibitions today due to global and instantaneous reporting.

The transgressions committed in our own backyards appear to pale in exposure and significance with similar events occurring elsewhere. These events, though abstract and geographically distant, are magnified by the intensity of news and social media exposure. Atrocities may still shock and can provoke wrath. We may not physically participate in the outrage but often concur with appropriate revenge.

On national and even international calamities, high-profile television commentators, social activists and political leaders seize these moments to espouse their specific bias, causes or indignation. Their fury often appears more opportunistic than genuine.

Compare the intensity of this anger with local tragedies before global viewing.

San Jose in 1933 was a modest community of approximately 60,000 despite having the distinction of being California's first state capital. The entirety of its county, Santa Clara, which encompasses the majority of contemporary Silicon Valley, boasted only 150,000 residents in the 1930 census.

Today the population of San Jose hovers near one million, surpassing San Francisco as the state's third largest urban center. Aside from the change and challenges growth necessitates, citizen involvement has become more neighborhood oriented and with the commuting sector, nearly nonexistent.

In 1933, San Jose's major shopping source, Hart's Department Store was located on the southeastern corner of Market and Santa Clara Streets downtown. Giant department stores in the 1930s (until the 1960s) were the shopping and social Mecca before urban decentralization and multi-store shopping malls. The Hart family was well respected locally and wealthy but not considered pretentious. They represented examples to be emulated back when role models still mattered.

Patriarch Leopold Hart had established a dry cleaning operation in San Jose originally in 1866. The family operations expanded and thrived under his son Alex J. Hart, Sr. who founded the flagship store in 1902. His eldest 22-year-old son Brooke was being groomed to replace him. He was employed at the store as an Assistant Department Manager.

Brooke Hart had distinguished himself with his studies at Bellarmine College Preparatory and by earning a degree from Santa Clara University. He effortlessly assumed the role of *Golden Boy* and was the town's most eligible and desirable bachelor. His wavy blond hair, blue eyes and handsome appearance were coupled by an engaging personality. He personified the qualities most parents would envy in their children.

He was a trusted and responsible individual serving as the designated chauffeur for his father who had never learned to drive. His 1933 green Studebaker roadster was renowned as one of only two models navigating San Jose roads. It was difficult to imagine anything but success and prosperity for his future.

Then fate intervened. Local kidnappers abducted him.

In 1933, the United States was mired in the Great Depression. The country limped forward in economic agony, shouldering the burden of overwhelming economic stress, unemployment and disillusionment. The accumulating malaise remained pent-up and ready for expression. San Jose would manifest an eruption of this frustration.

Charles Lindbergh, Jr., the year and a half old son of the famed aviator had been abducted on the evening of March 1, 1932. Two months later, his body was discovered with a crushed skull. The nation's eyes were riveted in horror at the unfolding search, arrest, trial and execution of the convicted kidnapper, Bruno Hauptmann. Was he guilty based on the slim circumstantial evidence? Or did the actual kidnapper, a rumored acquaintance, set him up for the crime?

He maintained his innocence until his execution. Trial procedures and evidence became questionable once the verdict was announced. Some suggest that Hauptmann's German ancestry made him an ideal candidate for conviction based on the tide of popular opinion following World War I. Hauptman's widow fought vehemently but unsuccessfully for nearly sixty years to re-open the case until her death in 1994.

Brooke Hart was not a helpless infant. His popularity, kidnapping and brutal death equally stirred local passions and a response to excess. Newspaper and radio reports blatantly convicted two individuals for the crime without the benefit of a public trial. The media's utter bias towards their guilt and demands for immediate retribution incited a brazen public act that seems incredulous today...a public lynching.

Lynchings were not foreign to the California system of justice. They were employed throughout the nineteenth and early twentieth century as frontier justice. By the 1930s, they tended to be regarded as barbaric public expressions of revenge.

A significant number of San Jose residents ignored the shifting interpretation. The public hanging was a popularly supported display.

It is arguable that the culprits did or didn't deserve their swift justice. If found guilty, their actions would have likely merited the death penalty. But the most obvious lingering question was whether they were indeed guilty. Both perpetrators, John Maurice Holmes and Harold Thurman were judged based on conflicting evidence and potentially forced confessions.

The Constitutional sixth amendment, which in all criminal prosecutions guarantees the right of a speedy and public trial, was discarded. Vigilantes replaced the role of a jury.

Newspapers and radio from the outset explicitly documented the gruesome events behind Brooke Hart's kidnapping. Nearing 5 p.m. on November 9th, Brooke was exiting a parking garage behind his father's store with the intent of driving him to a planned civic event.

According to media reports, two men appearing armed approached him as he slowed his car. He was forced to drive to another location where the kidnappers switched vehicles. The threesome then drove to the western entrance of the San Mateo Bridge.

In 1933, the bridge was a privately owned tollway and the longest in the world. The original span was principally a two-lane causeway trestle. The bridge was neither profitable nor well traveled. Traffic did not exceed 2,000 cars per day until 1947. A modern publicly financed replacement opened in 1967 to accommodate increased traffic. A section of the original western approach remains beside the replacement bridge. It was renamed the Werder Fishing Pier in 1968.

Later during the evening of the abduction, Hart was reportedly bound with baling wire that was attached to concrete blocks. He was repeatedly bashed over the skull with these same blocks and dumped over the railing into the frigid Bay waters. Neither the violent beating nor cold initially submerged him.

Instead he flayed violently and screamed for assistance. The kidnappers had neglected to account for the low tide conditions. As Hart flailed and refused to sink beneath the surface, they began repeatedly shooting at him until he was silenced.

One may assume the combination of the bullet wounds, hyperventilation and beating trauma ultimately lapsed him into unconsciousness and drowning. The autopsy however indicated that no bullets had penetrated Hart's body.

Was the media chronological account accurate or fanciful speculation?

Upon the assumption of their victim's apparent death, one kidnapper drove to San Francisco that evening to telephone the Hart family twice with exorbitant ransom demands. Another account had the telephone calls originating from downtown San Jose pay phones located within one half mile of each other.

Ransom letters were reported to have been simultaneously mailed with postmarks from both Sacramento and Los Angeles. The deception was to confuse the police.

Police were stationed at the Hart's residence and their phones were tapped. Following the kidnapper's original calls on the evening of the abduction, renewed contact with the family followed five days later.

The abductor's capture followed an odd and almost incredulous storyline. Harold Thurmond was caught making a ransom demand from a San Jose hotel and parking garage pay phone. The phone in question was located a mere 150 feet from the San Jose Police headquarters. Could a kidnapper potentially be this incompetent and stupid? Or was the account an invented narrative?

Thurmond fingered John Holmes as his co-conspirator. In the course of separate interrogations, each provided conflicting details regarding Hart's kidnapping, the vehicle transfer and clumsy killing. Both signed written confessions implicating the other as the principle culprit. The confessions may have been valid but the operating procedures employed by investigators were suspect.

Upon the pair's capture and confession, the family was notified of their son's official death. His body still eluded police. The waters around the bridge were dragged without success for twelve days. San Jose residents waited impatiently. The confessed kidnappers were temporarily relocated from downtown San Jose to San Francisco's Potrero Hill police station. Authorities feared trouble with the mounting public anger and hysteria over the case. Their suspicions proved prophetic.

Two duck hunters discovered Brooke Hart's partially dressed and decomposed body on November 26th, just south of the bridge.

With the discovery, residents were once again stunned into revulsion over the horror and enormity of the act. Shock was transformed into rage and demands for revenge. In newspapers, there was zero column lineage reserved towards any expression of doubt or presumption of innocence. Blatant suggestions of impending mob justice made the act inevitable. The wait proved abbreviated.

Despite their probable guilt based on the discovered location of the body, the legal case against Thurmond and Holmes was far from conclusive. Their signed confessions may have conceivably been discredited by a shrewd legal defense given the questionable circumstances behind obtaining them. Prior to the establishment of Miranda Rights protection, guaranteeing legal representation upon request, forced confessions were often beaten out of suspects when evidence was marginal.

Factual discrepancies in the account of events and the dubious mental capabilities of the accused would have raised probable doubts regarding guilt or innocence.

More tellingly, there were only two confirmed eyewitnesses to any aspect of the kidnapping. A couple, who managed the San Jose Country Club, witnessed a passenger exchange between Hart's Studebaker and another sedan, which they significantly misidentified. They further claimed to have witnessed five men involved in the transfer of Hart. In the FBI kidnapping file released 50 years later under the Freedom of Information Act, five not two unidentified males were sought as responsible parties.

San Jose residents were unwilling to settle for anything less than swift blood revenge. Their attitude then is in sharp contrast with today's extended trials and appeal process that often lengthen the guilty into an advanced age.

Judgment should have been suspended until the facts were conclusive to make a clear decision. The San Jose citizenry rushed to a frenzied judgment based on raw emotion and absent of confirmed proof. Resolution and closure, even for such a heinous action as a kidnapping demands thorough proof and due process.

We will never know for certain if the mob's instincts were accurate. Their fury eliminated the opportunity for complete disclosure. A similar killing would mirror this rashness thirty years later by an individual reacting to another national tragedy.

On November 24, 1963, Jack Ruby liquidated suspected presidential assassin Lee Harvey Oswald during his Dallas Police Station transfer. President John Kennedy had been killed the day before and the world reeled in collective shock. Upon Oswald's killing, many applauded Ruby's apparent spontaneous patriotic gesture of revenge. Over time his own motives became suspect. His act eliminated the sole individual who might have shed legitimate light on what had transpired the day before. Oswald was gone and conspiracy theories have multiplied since.

Americans lost their best opportunity for disclosure and healing.

Few today regard Jack Ruby as a patriot. Instead he has assumed the role of impediment to inquiry, truth and justice. He died incarcerated in 1967 of cancer, rationalizing the impulsive nature of his action. He perished as a pathetically forgotten historical footnote.

Whether Thurmond and Holmes were ultimately innocent or guilty became irrelevant on Sunday evening November 27, 1933.

Inflammatory reporting during the preceding week suggested the assumed killers, back in San Jose custody, might avert prosecution because of their defective confessions, no eyewitnesses and suspect evidence.

Published accounts inferred they were consulting with a highly renowned San Francisco lawyer and were contemplating an insanity plea, thus evading capital punishment. Since that original article appeared, both men were subsequently declared legally sane by evaluating medical examiners invalidating such an option. This detail remained conveniently unreported by the press,

Absent of this confirmation, any suggestion of an alternative to a death sentence was considered unacceptable by the populous. Innocent blood had been shed and expeditious retribution was the only appropriate response.

The discovery of Hart's body galvanized action the following fateful day. The prisoners were interned at the Santa Clara County Courthouse across the street from St. James Park downtown. The park today is an idle green oasis dwarfed by an expanding base of commercial and condominium high-rises. The benches and shaded trees accommodate transients and the homeless, ignored amongst San Jose's upwardly mobile. The park's prominence has become as forgotten as giant department stores, public lynchings and the interrupted legacy of Brooke Hart.

The swelling crowd lingering across the street from the jail alarmed County Sheriff Willia Emig. He telephoned California Governor James Rolph requesting that the National Guard be deployed to protect the prisoners. Rolph refused and further confirmed that he would pardon any participating members involved in the hanging.

The lynching, repeatedly suggested by newspapers and radio as a probable outcome, became fact. Their view was that any potential travesty of justice enabling the accused to escape punishment was to be prevented at all costs. Their own sensationalism instigated a farce of equal proportion.

The mob was estimated by press outlets to range anywhere between five to fifteen thousand local men, women and children. Reporters, cameramen and live radio broadcasts were poised and positioned to recount the impending spectacle. They were neither premature nor disappointed.

As the darkness descended, outnumbered sheriff's deputies fired tear gas into the crowd attempting to disperse them. Predictably, the crowd's numbers only expanded and anger intensified. A nearby construction site was raided to locate a battering ram and at approximately 9:00 p.m., an assault began. A furious group successfully broke down the doors and stormed the jail.

Sheriff Emig abandoned the bottom two floors of the jail where Thurmond and Holmes were being held. The mob leaders manhandled the partially clad prisoners whose fate was assured. Neither had yet been formally charged or indicted.

The two were expediently hung on a convenient park tree while the throng applauded. The spectacle might have easily resembled an 18th century French Revolution guillotine parties. The hanging images were explicitly broadcast throughout the United States. They still shock today. Both men swung freely with total frontal exposure and their genitals protruding.

The employed gallows tree was initially preserved to serve as a public caution against capital offenses. Souvenir hunters hacked, stripped bark and retained branches as mementos. The city council ultimately decided to cut it down due to its notoriety. Several comparably aged trees remain in St. James Park, statuesque witnesses to a historical anomaly.

It is difficult to feel sympathy for Thurmond and Holmes, particularly if they were guilty. The slaying of Brooke Hart was a profound tragedy and a loss the community legitimately mourned because of his personal and his family's decency.

Too many perpetrators continue to evade prompt justice and punishment. Their examples become an affront to our system of justice. Perhaps each of us would have identified and participated with the lynching if we were intimately affected by Hart's death.

For each survivor and victim's family that has had to experience the loss of a loved one, the impulse towards revenge is normal and difficult to repress. Over eight decades have passed since a fateful evening when righteous indignation overwhelmed the potentially arctic paced due process of our court system.

PHOTOS: Site of former Hart's Department Store, Site of garage where Brooke was kidnapped, Three perspectives of the the old San Mateo Bridge (where Brooke hart's body was dumped) and the adjacent newer bridge replacement, Santa Clara County Courthouse and Jail, St. James Park where the hanging occurred

Brook Hart Shooting and Body Dump:
San Francisco Bay waters below the western entrance
railing to the former San Mateo Bridge (later renamed
the Werder Fishing Pier)

340

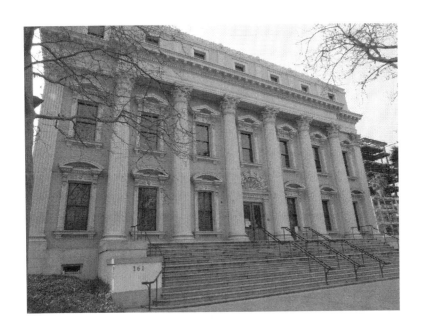

**Brook Hart's Kidnappers Public Lynching:
St. James Park, North Second Street, San Jose**

Cameron's Pub and a Stiff Dose of Cabrillo Highway History

Cameron's Pub located along a coastal stretch of Cabrillo Highway (101), features two authentic parked London double-decker buses in their parking lot. Their addition accentuates the English themed ambiance boasting a colorful history.

Over the course of a century, the pub and upstairs rooms have served as brothels on at least three occasions. During Prohibition, bootleggers brewed their inventory in the canyons of Half Moon Bay and deposited their loads at the facility for redistribution to San Francisco Speakeasy's. Legendary gun exchanges between bootleggers, hijackers and law enforcement historically rattled the neighboring highway corridors. Gangster Al Capone's sister reportedly owned the slot machines once employed on site.

Three escaped convicts from San Quentin arrived one evening in the 1930s. Only one left after shooting the other two during a dispute. During World War II, the army took over the Inn employing the downstairs as a mess hall and the upstairs for officers' quarters.

During the post war years, stories have been passed down regarding drunken bartenders taking turns shooting pistols at targets set up on the wall opposite the bar. In the 60s, an impatient Hell's Angels gang rode their motorcycles into the bar to place expedient orders.

Celebrity sightings are frequent. Even if the history and accompanying tales steer towards exaggeration, the English themed novelty merits a cold pint for contemplation.

Cameron's Pub:
1410 South Cabrillo Highway, Half Moon Bay

Kohl Mansion: A Cursed Owner Terminates His Claim

Nestled amidst the serenity of groomed lawns, statuesque trees and Mercy High School in Burlingame, the Kohl Mansion rises in Arthurian splendor, timeless and seemingly ageless. The original builder and owner was Charles Frederick *Freddie* Kohl, son of William H, Kohl, a pioneer Alaskan ship builder and fur trader. The property was purchased in 1874 from William Polhemus, considered the father of San Mateo.

Originally known as *The Oaks*, the 63-room red-brick Tudor mansion rests on forty pastoral acres. Initially constructed in 1915, the estate features an expansive English rose garden, tennis courts, green houses, large carriage house and a 150,000-gallon reservoir.

Freddie Kohl was schooled at the prestigious Swarthmore College in Pennsylvania, but returned to the San Francisco Peninsula and quickly established himself as a popular figure in San Francisco society.

In 1896, he married Elizabeth Dunlop, but the union was doomed by her death from appendicitis in 1900. Four years later, he wed songstress Mary Elizabeth *Bessie* Godly. The same year, his father died and Freddie inherited the estate grounds. For the first five years, the marriage appeared sound.

In 1908, Freddie hired an emotionally unstable young French maid named Adele Verge. On a family trip to Southern California the year following, she became involved in a physical altercation with the chauffeur. Freddie sided with the chauffeur and had her arrested and psychiatrically evaluated. Following her release, Verge sued Kohl for slander, false arrest and imprisonment.

The trial took place in 1911 and the predictable outcome favored Kohl. Adele administered her own form of justice by shooting Freddie outside of the courthouse with a nickel-plated revolver following the verdict. The bullet lodged too close to his heart to risk surgery. He recovered but the impact would haunt him for the remainder of his life.

Adele Verge was deported to France and instituted to an asylum. She vowed retribution towards Freddie who recognized the legitimacy of the threat.

Freddie and Bessie returned to the Kohl Estate in 1914 and moved into the completed mansion the following year. The location became a high society fixture for parties and events. Superficially everything appeared back to normal. The reality was far different.

The shooting tormented Freddie and as his accompanying depression, jealousy towards Bessie and paranoia worsened. His outbursts became intolerable. Within a few years, Bessie had endured enough and left. She toured with the Red Cross to entertain World War I troops. The couple never divorced nor reconciled.

Freddie acquired a lover, Marion Louderback Lord and moved into the St. Francis Hotel in San Francisco with her. His emotional instability peaked when he heard rumors that Adele Verge had been released from the French asylum.

On November 23, 1921 after suffering a stroke, Freddie shot himself fatally in the skull at the Del Monte Lodge near Pebble Beach. The bulk of his inheritance went to his mistress including *The Oaks* mansion.

Marion Louderback Lord had no interest in a household that had brought no one happiness and sold the property to the Sisters of Mercy in 1924. The initial local reaction seemed bizarre.

In 1925, a local chapter of the Ku Klux Klan in hooded regalia descended upon the convent, honking their car horns, shouting oaths and reportedly burning a cross above the Mother Superior's house. As with the majority of this organization's activities, their precise intent was unknown.

Sightings of spirits and unexplainable evidence of white starchy powder spooked the nuns. Two priests conducted a secret 1927 ritual blessing and exorcism.

The mansion has since settled into more conventional acceptance serving as the film setting for Mary Pickford's *Little Lord Fauntleroy*, Robin William's *Flubber* and various scheduled weddings, concerts and social gatherings.

Kohl Mansion: 2750 Adeline Drive, Burlingame

Moss Beach Distillery: The Return of the Blue Lady

Frank Torres opened the Moss Beach Distillery along the San Mateo Coast in 1927 catering to celebrated Silent Era film stars, gangsters and San Francisco politicians. Mystery writer Dashiell Hammett *(Sam Spade, The Maltese Falcon)* was a regular client and immortalized the restaurant's setting in one of his detective stories.

The restaurant, perched on the cliffs of a then secluded beach became an ideal Speakeasy establishment with its adjacent location to a landing spot for Canadian rumrunners during Prohibition. Under cover of the habitual fog and nightfall, illegal whiskey would be dragged up the steep cliffs and transported to waiting vehicles bound for San Francisco.

Torres's social and political connections enabled the Moss Beach Distillery to avoid being raided throughout the course of Prohibition. Following its 1933 conclusion, Torres converted the establishment into a successful restaurant, which it remains today.

One of his most famous and enduring customers is the ill-fated *Blue Lady*, an apparition named Mary Ellen haunting the premises. There are two conflicting accounts of her demise. The first involves her extramarital affair with *Speakeasy* pianist John Contina. The couple would rendezvous at a hotel next door to the Distillery following extended moonlit strolls along Moss Beach. In this account, Mary Ellen was confronted during one of these promenades by her jealous husband and stabbed repeatedly. Cortina survived the attack and judiciously disappeared.

John Cortina was rumored to be conducting an affair with a second woman at the same time named Anna Philbrick. She reported jumped off the Moss Beach cliffs and drowned when informed of his duplicity.

The tariff for infidelity proved steep for the supposedly vanishing Cortina. His body later washed up on the beach, a consequence of his acknowledged deceit.

A second more banal story is that Mary Ellen died in an automobile accident during a severe storm. Generations of owners, patrons and employees have reported sighting the *Blue Lady*. Her actions have included moving objects, whisperings, cash register malfunctions, and physical touching.

Moss Beach Distillery
140 Beach Way, Moss Beach

Half Moon Bay's Ocean Beach Hotel: A Shrouded but Panoramic Past

Fiery redhead Maymie Cowley operated the Ocean Beach Hotel (later renamed the Miramar Restaurant) from 1918 until 1955. Ever the opportunist, Cowley unapologetically managed the property as a roadhouse Speakeasy during Prohibition offering storage capacity for illegal liquor, gambling outlets and prostitution in the upstairs room. Ten small rooms accommodated customers. Each was equipped with a bell system connected to the kitchen below enabling convenient food service.

Half Moon Bay was an ideal location for the transfer of illegal liquor cargo and access to San Francisco. During Maymie's reign, her roadhouse was raided numerous times. The interior featured revolving kitchen cabinets and other secret compartments designed to conceal the contraband.

Maymie Cowley lived on site for 40 years. It was rumored that she was involved in knife fights at other bars. She moved across the hill in 1955 after a burglar broke into her bedroom and attacked her. The intruder entered with his face masked and hovered over her bed. At 80, the wildcat did not succumb passively. He felt compelled to fire a gun into the wall, broke her glasses and left her with nose and shoulder injuries. His reward was $75 hidden in her cigar box.

The Ocean Beach offered then as now a stunning panorama of the Pacific Ocean. The contemporary scene today is viewable via a patio expansion complete with accommodating firepit and glass barrier windbreak. Today's tamer Half Moon Bay environment has evolved with fresh residential development and more congenial hospitality. The formerly isolated village has begun to morph territorially with neighboring Pacifica. All that remains from its former turbulent era is the fog, which habitually shrouds the community and distant horizon.

Ocean Beach Hotel (Renamed Miramar Beach Restaurant): 131 Mirada Road, Half Moon Bay

PG & E's San Bruno Pipeline Explosion: The Vulnerability Beneath Us

Near the intersection of Glenview Drive and Earl Avenue in suburban San Bruno are two nondescript serene park areas. One features a basketball court and the other children's climbing stations, terraced landscaping and several sitting benches. Each bench has an attached bronze placard inscribed with a memorial name. One bench has three names, representing three generations of the Bullis family.

There is little to hint at the origins necessitating each park's creation nor the significance of the eight names. Their creation followed an unforeseen combustible explosion. On the evening of September 9, 2010 just after 6 p.m., the neighborhood resembled a war zone.

A 30-inch diameter steel natural gas pipeline owned by power utility Pacific Gas and Electric Company (PG &E) abruptly exploded into flames in this Crestmoor residential neighborhood. The roar and trembling resembled an earthquake or even a jet airline crashing from nearby San Francisco Airport two miles away. Eyewitnesses to the explosion reported the initial blast as releasing a wall of flames more than 1,000 feet high.

The epicenter at Glenview Drive and Earl Avenue became a crater 167 feet long, 26 feet wide and 40 feet deep. Neighboring homes became engulfed in fire. Thirty-eight would ultimately be destroyed or demolished. Eight people were killed (the names on the park benches) and many additionally suffered burns from an inferno that lasted eighteen hours before being fully contained.

The conclusion as to the cause revealed the pipeline might have been improperly installed. Foul play and terrorism were ruled out following a San Bruno Police investigation. The segment of pipe that blew out onto the street was 28 feet long. An inspection of the severed pipe revealed that it had been composed of smaller section welded together with a seam running along its length. The pipeline had been installed in 1956 and current X-ray testing methods were not available to detect defective welds at that time.

Three years later, PG & E settled legal claims with 347 victims and announced in their 2015 annual report that they had paid out $558 million in third-party claims, $92 million in legal expenses, and received $515 million from insurance. Customers settled the discrepancy through higher rates.

PG & E has endured a woeful twenty-first century. In 2015, the Public Utilities Commission fined the company $1.8 billion. A series of safety calamities and adverse judgments promoted the company to file for bankruptcy in January 2019.

The San Bruno disaster has become their highest profile incident, but may foretell a grim future. The network of California fault lines, discovered, hidden and submerged creates a hazardous vulnerability that the next massive earthquake may awaken.

PG & E Pipeline Explosion:
Epicenter: Corner of Glenview Drive And Earl Avenue,
San Bruno

357

Sam's Castle: Eclectic Suburban Royalty

Henry Harrison McCloskey was a San Francisco attorney horrifically frightened by the 1906 Earthquake and Fire. He addressed his fears in the most rationale fashion by constructing a castle on a cliff in nearby Pacifica overlooking the ocean. The structure featured turrets and battlements, dense walls, steel reinforcement and a menacing barricade.

His precautions succeeded. The castle remained despite McCloskey's death a decade later. His grandson became former Congressional representative Pete McCloskey.

The castle assumed new ownership upon his death to a man named Galen Hickok, a charlatan doctor who converted the premises into an abortion clinic. He was arrested for his activities and sentenced to five years in San Quentin. His son, Max, took over his abortion practice and followed the identical fate as his father. Ownership changed once more to a Montana miner who purchased the castle and converted it into an infinitely more respectable Speakeasy and brothel during Prohibition.

Next a religious couple reformed the premises into a center for the Red Cross employing the large ballrooms and drawing rooms for events. During World War II, the couple leased it to the Coast Guard who stationed more than 20 sailors, officers and their German shepherds in the castle. The military tenants shredded the facility and it remained abandoned for a decade afterwards.

The properties savior and ultimate namesake, Sam Mazza, arrived and purchased the property in 1959. Mazza was a painting contractor who worked in several of San Francisco's old theatres. Over the succeeding forty years, he littered the property with suits of armor, swords, busts of Greek gods, Virgin Mary statues, a throne, coats of arms and whatever suited his whimsical fancy. He installed stained glass windows.

Sam Mazza was the life of any party and extravagant meals, dancing complete with crowns became staples of his *joie de vivre*. The world lost a beloved merrymaker when he passed away in 2002. The castle was deeded to a foundation upon his death, which has financed reparations to the building, sorted through his treasures and begun conducting low-scale public tours.

The sheer magnitude and audacity of the property seems foreign to Pacifica and the present era. The roadway ascent to Sam's fabled perch may seem treacherous, but it is merely a caution to frighten away timid and mediocre spirits. Extravagance and kitsch ultimately prevail in this four-story, 24-room kingdom.

Sam's Castle:
900 Mirador Terrace, Pacifica

Sanchez Adobe: The Taming and Neutering of the Wild West

On the North Bank of San Pedro Creek, Francisco Sanchez, Commandant of the San Francisco Presidio was awarded a land grant by the government of Mexico in 1839. He built the Sanchez Adobe with bricks from the 1786 constructed *San Pedro y Sam Pablo Asistencia*, an outpost designed for farming and missionary work attached to San Francisco's Mission Dolores. *Rancho San Pedro* as it was originally known was completed in 1846.

With the arrival and annexation by the American government, the property changed hands to Edward Kirkpatrick in 1871. He remodeled the Adobe structure extensively throughout the late 1880s. The building served a variety of purposes with a division into twenty rooms. The structure was called the *Adobe House* and featured an accommodating brothel. During Prohibition, it seamlessly added a Speakeasy created a full service package. Eventually, the Adobe became a farm building associated with the artichoke industry in the San Pedro Valley during the 1940s.

The County of San Mateo purchased the Sanchez Adobe and surrounding 5 1/2 acres in 1947 and began a comprehensive restoration process that was initially completed in 1953. Work has recently resumed to upgrade the facility with scant mention of its more decadent past.

**Sanchez Adobe/San Pedro Hotel:
1000 Linda Mar Boulevard, Pacifica**

San Mateo County Courthouse and the Surprise Family Probate

In 1858, S. M. Mezes donated landed to San Mateo County and by December, the first courthouse had been constructed. In 1868, an earthquake caused the second floor of the building to be removed. A new courthouse was constructed in 1882 and modernized in 1905 in the Roman and Renaissance revival styles.

One year later, the building was demolished by the San Francisco Earthquake raising questions regarding construction practices and shortcuts taken by the contractors. Only the dome structure survived.

In 1910, a renovated and more earthquake resilient courthouse was completed with a similar design to the 1905 version. The structure remains today absent of a 1939 annex. A 2006 reconstruction project returned the courthouse entry portico and façade back to the 1910 design featuring stately columns, eagle sculptures and fountains making it more community accessible.

In 1998, the San Mateo Courthouse operations transferred to another Redwood City location and the historic courthouse became the San Mateo County History Museum.

The historic courthouse has remained essentially scandal free and the site of many notable court cases. One of the more notable historic probate trials involved the 1920 will of Henry Pike Bowie.

Henry was the third husband of Agnes Poet Howard, many years his senior. She had accumulated a significant estate from marriage to two former husbands who happened to be brothers. She left one-fifth of her estate to Bowie upon her death in 1893 and the balance to her adult children.

Bowie was an attorney but filed only a single brief during his career. He sued the town of Burlingame when the local marshal impounded some of his cows from his Severn Dairy Farm. He lived a comfortable existence and was a member of the Burlingame Country Club and San Mateo Polo Club. He dabbled in leisure pursuits including gardening and art patronage.

He honed his interests towards Japanese art becoming an acknowledged authority on the subject. His passion took him to Japan on numerous occasions, which raised no suspicions. On his final visit to Japan in 1918, he was sent as a special emissary for the U.S. State Department. He returned in 1920, two months before his death.

In January 1921, Bowie's handwritten will went into probate. Specific sums were allotted to his sister and two brothers. The remainder of his fortune was split between his third brother and Koma Hirano, Imao Hirano and Takeo Hirano of Yokohama, Japan.

The Japanese trio was revealed to be his wife and two sons.

Apparently no one in Burlingame realized he was living a dual existence, although it was apparently well known in Yokohama that he was head of a household.

The news shocked the community and even more so one of his stepsons, George Howard. He filed a suit in the San Mateo courthouse to nullify the will. He claimed the Hiranos had been exclusively Bowie's hosts and they had used undue influence to secure their designated share. He further claimed that Bowie was mentally impaired and since the money had originated from his mother, the Howard family was entitled to it.

Wisely, presiding Judge Buck tossed the lawsuit and the Hiranos were granted their entitled inheritance.

San Mateo County Courthouse Building
2200 Broadway, Redwood City

A High Voltage Grand Finale for Promoter Bill Graham

Sixty-year old Bill Graham (born Wulf Wolodia Grajonca) was a legendary Bay Area rock concert promoter perpetually in transit and hurried. Moving to San Francisco in 1965, he managed his initial series of entertainment performances with the San Francisco Mime Troupe.

He began staging benefit free concerts that ultimately blossomed into some of the world's largest scale outdoor performances. Graham was recognized for tirelessly promoting and cultivating acts such as the Grateful Dead, Santana, Jefferson Airplane, Janis Joplin, Elvin Bishop, Tower of Power, Eddie Money and Journey. He operated the bi-coastal Fillmore East and West Auditoriums and was directly involved in concert ticket distribution.

Regionally, his legendary *Day on the Green* bookings staged between 1973 and the early 1990s within the Oakland Coliseum featured multiple bands of legendary caliber performing within a single day. The combined quality and reputation of the participating bands seems incomprehensible today.

Acts and events booked through the Shoreline Amphitheatre and/or Concord Pavilion were promoted through his *Bill Graham Presents* operation. He owned *The Punch Line*, *Old Waldorf* and *Wolfgang's* clubs in San Francisco. He spun gold from his licensing, iconic concert posters, t-shirt and merchandising operations. His promotional reach monopolized the San Francisco Bay Area music scene.

At the apex of his ascension and ambitions, all abruptly ceased.

On October 25, 1991, Graham's life and professional legacy literally crashed en route to flying to his Novato home following a *Huey Lewis and the News* concert at the Concord Pavilion. His sole purpose for attending was to secure Lewis' commitment to perform in a future benefit concert for victims of a 1991 Oakland hills fire.

That evening's torrential gusts and rain created severe flying conditions. His transporting Bell Jet Ranger helicopter strayed off course and flew too low over the tidal marshlands north of the San Pablo Bay near the confluence of the Solano, Napa and Sonoma county borders. The aircraft errantly smashed into a 223-foot high-voltage tower stationed at Vista Point along Sears Point Highway 37. The helicopter incinerated immediately killing Graham, his girlfriend Melissa Gold and pilot Steve Kahn (who was posthumously blamed). The *Huey Lewis* concert was interrupted due to a resulting power surge and over 23,000 home were left without power until morning. The charred helicopter remained hung, attached and suspended for over a day until a large crane could remove and lower it to the ground.

Following his death, management of *Bill Graham Presents* was assumed by a group of employees including his sons. This new collective eventually sold the company, which has subsequently been dismantled. The diminutive San Francisco Civic Auditorium was renamed the *Bill Graham Civic Auditorium* in his honor.

The damaged tower and helicopter were unsalvageable. A replacement tower was installed. Any solitary individual will almost certainly never replicate the scope and extent of Bill Graham's Bay Area empire.

**Helicopter Crash Replacement Tower:
Vista Point adjacent to Highway 37, six miles west of
Vallejo**

Jurgensen Saloon/Lido Bar: Respite for a Future Writer

Constructed in 1847, George Jurgensen operated a saloon near the foot of First Street during the 1880s frequented by a prolific but yet unknown writer named Jack London. The author remained a lifelong patron and lived for a period nearby in a houseboat on the Benicia waterfront. He never forgot the influence of the tavern towards his future licentious existence immortalizing the saloon in his story *John Barleycorn*. London took solace not only with Jurgensen's generous pourings, but paid female companionship upstairs. The building continued operations throughout the Second World War managed by Madam Gertie Gallardo. Jack London's life may have flamed out by forty, but the Lido has been relocated and reincarnated five blocks uptown currently as a spiritualist oriented gift shop.

**Jurgensen Saloon/Lido Bar:
501 First Street, Benicia**

California State Capital Experiment and the Washington House

It is difficult to imagine a sparsely populated California era when compared with the colossus that it has evolved into today. Between February 1853 and 1854, the entire state capitol operations were housed in a diminutive Benicia mansion only four years following American statehood.

The Benicia location experiment followed two failed attempts to host the capitol building in adjacent Vallejo. The sites were selected because the grounds had been donated to the state by landowner Mariano Guadalupe Vallejo, a former Republic of Mexico officer attempting to solidify his status and ingratiate him with the new American overseers.

Poor weather, inadequate structures, uncomfortable sleeping quarters compounded by howling hillside coyotes had doomed Vallejo' hosting tenure. Seating furniture consisted of wooden barrels and constant ceiling dripping during winter. A basement saloon provided marginal diversion, but generated minimal legislative progress.

Benicia's longevity fared no better, lasting only a single year. The building, originally the town's city hall, however proved a substantial improvement. In 1854, despite intense opposition by local residents, the legislature, governor, and upscaled building furnishings were loaded on board a steamship bound for Sacramento. So vehement were the local commercial protests, the boat initially was not permitted to dock for loading purposes until a ransom was paid. This extortion was refused and ship ultimately relocated to another local wharf.

The Washington House was constructed in 1850-51 and

originally located at the East Fifth Street wharf. The structure served as a residence for some members of the California state legislature while Benicia was the capital city. The building was relocated to the present site in 1856. Uses have included a brothel, newspaper publishing office, butcher shop, dry good store, Chinese lottery, restaurant and speak easy during prohibition days.

**Benicia State Capital Building:
115 West G Street, Benicia**

Washington House: 333 First Street, Benicia

The Zodiac: The Taunting Killer

The most notorious serial killer in Northern California operated in the late 1960s and early 1970s. His legacy began violently in my hometown of Vallejo, California.

On December 20, 1968 along an isolated stretch of Lake Herman Road, two high school acquaintances of my older sister, Betty Lou Jensen and David Faraday were viciously murdered shortly after 11 p.m. The couple was on their first date together. Lake Herman Road was a diversion from their original plans of a high school Christmas concert.

They wanted time alone. Instead, they became the victims of a cowardly execution.

For approximately 45 minutes prior to the shooting, Faraday parked his mother's Rambler in a gravel turnout, a well-known spot for intimacy. Another vehicle pulled up beside. The killer exited and ordered the couple out of the car. Jensen exited first and when Faraday was halfway out, the killer shot him directly in the skull.

Fleeing towards the main road from the killer in the open gravel turnout instead of veering towards potentially protective shrubbery, Jensen was gunned down twenty-eight feet from the car by five shots through her back. The killer had taped a flashlight atop his gun for sighting purposes in the pitch dark. After convinced that both of his victims were dead, he drove off. The execution was completed within a ten-minute gap before a passing vehicle stopped.

This murder began the first in a series of attacks and fortuitous escapes by the Zodiac killer.

The reaction about the first killings within the community was stunned silence and disbelief. The viciousness and arbitrary nature of the murders forever destroyed a local sense of security that residents shared. Speculation initially focused on individuals who might have had a motive for killing either of the two victims. Soon it became apparent there was neither motive nor probable suspect within the couple's circle of acquaintances.

The Zodiac struck again a half-year later less than four miles away.

Around midnight on July 4, 1969, Darlene Ferrin and Michael Mageau drove into the Blue Rock Springs Parking lot, a popular local recreational facility. As with the earlier murder, a car drove up beside the couple. Initially it didn't linger, but immediately drove off. Returning 10 minutes later, the driver parked directly behind them and left his vehicle.

Mageau, still living today, claimed on numerous occasions that Ferrin might have been familiar with the driver. He approached the passenger side door of Ferrin's car carrying a flashlight and 9 mm Lugar. He blinded both occupants with the flashlight beam. He fired five times. Ferrin was killed instantly. Mageau miraculously survived despite sustaining wounds in his face, neck and chest. He would become one of two Zodiac victim survivors.

Forty-five minutes later, the killer telephoned the Vallejo Police Department to claim responsibility for the attack as well as the killings six and a half months earlier. The call was placed only a few blocks from the police station. This bold taunting tactic would ultimately become an important element of the killer's terror scheme.

For then residents of Vallejo, the mention of Lake Herman Road and Blue Rock Springs Park could stimulate foreboding and nightmares.

What distinguished these homicides from comparable multiple murderers was that the killer chose his own identifying name. In a brazen series of letters sent to San Francisco Bay Area news outlets, he called himself *Zodiac*. Among these letters included four cryptograms. Of the four he mailed, only one was conclusively solved. The killer boasted that within their text, he had included his identity. Investigators have always doubted the accuracy of his claim.

What made the Zodiac ultimately globally recognized was that he was never apprehended. Significant law enforcement investigators and even speculating amateur sleuths have scoured details, published evidence, and varying theories for decades to no avail. Over the years, many suspects have been suggested and researched, but irrefutable evidence has never resulted in an indictment.

On August 1, 1969, the Zodiac killer began his correspondence with two newspapers, the *San Francisco Chronicle* and *Vallejo Times Herald* by mailing out identical letters establishing him as the source of the homicidal mayhem. Each guaranteed that subsequent killings would follow unless the text was published precisely as written. The newspapers obliged. A global media frenzy followed.

His pattern of boasting and taunting rhetoric would continue over the next five years resulting in innumerable false leads, inflated and false boasts by the killer, and massive speculation about his identity. To verify his credibility, the Zodiac included specific details about the murders, which had not yet been released to the public. In one letter, he would include a torn fragment from one of his shooting victim's bloodstained shirt.

Following his July 4th killing, he struck less than three months later.

On the afternoon of September 27, 1969, the Zodiac varied his killing method with a knife attack at Lake Berryessa in nearby Napa County. Two college students, Bryan Hartwell and Cecelia Shepard were idyllically picnicking when a man approached them wearing a black executioner's style hood and clip-on sunglasses over the eyeholes. The bizarre outfit included a bib-like device on his chest with a white 3x3" embroidered cross-circle symbol (resembling a target sight).

The man recounted a strange narrative to the couple about being an escaped convict in need of immediate cash and transportation. He claimed to be armed and convinced the pair to tie each other up. What they assumed to be a simple robbery turned grisly as he pulled out a knife and began stabbing both savagely and repeatedly. Thinking both were dead, the killer hiked 500 yards back to their vehicle. He drew the cross-circle symbol on Hartwell's car door with a black felt-tip pen and wrote beneath it the dates and locations of his previous killings.

At 7:40 p.m. the killer telephoned the Napa County Sheriff's office from a Napa pay telephone to report his latest double homicide. The receiver was found dangling off the hook only minutes later, a few blocks from the sheriff's office. A damp palm print was lifted from the receiver but never successfully matched with any later suspects.

What the Zodiac didn't realize when he placed the call 27 miles from the crime scene was that neither of his victims had yet expired from their wounds.

Cecelia Shepard was conscious when two Sheriff's deputies arrived, providing them with a detailed description of the attacker. Hartnell and Shepard were taken to a hospital in Napa by ambulance. Shepard lapsed into a coma during the transport and never regained consciousness. She died two days later. Hartnell survived to recount his tale and become the second survivor of the Zodiac.

The final documented killing occurred two weeks later on October 11, 1969. A lone passenger entered a taxi driven by Paul Stine at the intersection of Mason and Geary Streets in downtown San Francisco. He requested to be taken to the corner of Washington and Maple Streets in the city's Presidio Heights district.

Stine drove one block past Maple to Cherry Street for reasons that were never determined. The passenger then raised a 9mm pistol and shot Stine once in the back of his head. He then methodically removed Stine's wallet and car keys and tore away a section of Stine's bloodstained shirt. He wiped the interior of the cab before exiting towards the Presidio, a former military base, one block to the north.

Three teenagers observed the sequence of events across the street. At 9:55 p.m. they telephoned the police immediately after the crime had been committed. Two blocks away from the crime scene and responding to the police dispatch, a San Francisco policeman observed a Caucasian male strolling nonchalantly down the street before stepping into a nearby neighborhood stairwell.

The man was neither stopped nor questioned because the

police radio dispatcher had erroneously identified the potential suspect as an *African-American* male. The pedestrian was passed over. He vanished. Was he the Zodiac? In a later letter, the killer claimed *yes*.

The three teenage eyewitnesses collaborated with a police department artist to render a composite sketch that has become the sustaining image of the killer's portrait. Further police patrols that evening would produce no tangible suspects or leads.

The San Francisco, Napa County and Vallejo police departments assigned special investigators exclusively to the case. Yet there was minimal cooperation between them. Each department kept the investigative files closeted as each successive lead failed to conclusively produce a confirmed identity, arrest and closure. Many reasons have been cited for the failure of law enforcement officials to ultimately arrest a suspect who had left a preponderance of incriminating evidence. The San Francisco police department has claimed to have investigated over 2,500 suspect leads.

Among the most frequently cited criticisms voiced regarding the law enforcement investigation has been the poor cooperative efforts between police departments based on professional jealousies along with tainted and lost evidence. The most glaring reason however is that scientific forensic techniques and DNA comparative testing was non-existent during the late 1960s and 70s. The Zodiac was fortunate to have escaped both arrest and the advancement of technology.

Several letters, cards and cryptograms would follow during the subsequent years. The sources varied in terms of reliability. All reasonably credible correspondence abruptly ended in 1974.

The Zodiac, throughout the course of his writings, made numerous outrageous claims and threats. He threatened future massacres, terrorist activities to school buses, and to have even killed in excess of thirty victims. He pathetically claimed credit for unsolved crimes that received substantial media exposure. No substantive proof ever linked or confirmed his participation in any subsequent homicides beyond the five victims.

Most researchers and observers of this unsolved mystery have concluded that the actual Zodiac killer has been deceased for many years. There have been many explanations as to the reasons why he ultimately ceased his public communications. We may never know his identity. Websites, films, and books continue to be released suggesting fresh speculations and overlooked data. The law enforcement files still remain closed to public scrutiny.

What we do know is that his vicious unsolved killings and self-delusional correspondence traumatized many innocent citizens and irretrievably stained the topography of the San Francisco Bay area. Whatever renown or romantic allure the global media has attached to this iconic killer, the facts behind his acts ultimately proved far less glamorous.

Darlene Ferrin: Blue Rock Springs Park, Vallejo

Paul Stine: Corner of Washington and Cherry Streets, San Francisco

384

NAPA/SONOMA

Sonoma's Blue Wing Inn: A Historic Landmark On Wobbly Footing

The block-long adobe structure called the *Blue Wing Inn* is one of Sonoma's oldest constructions, adjacent to the downtown square. Designated as lot 35 on the settlement's earliest grid, the structure is located across the street from the former Mission San Francisco Solano's main building.

In the 1830s, Mariano Vallejo was named administrator to oversee the closing of the Spanish mission under the replacement Mexican governing authority. Vallejo granted the eastern half of lot 35 to Antonio Ortega, who was designated to handle day-to-day operations involved in the secular conversion of the former mission.

Ortega was reputed to be ruthless in his treatment of the local Native Americans and was removed from his position by Vallejo in 1837. He continued to live on the property and formulated his own secularization movement by operating a small tavern there until 1848.

In 1849, he sold the property to James C. Cooper and Thomas Spriggs. The pair immediately expanded construction to accommodate a ground level gambling hall and saloon. They added a second story enhanced by a wood-frame balcony and street access stairway. The rooms accommodated both overnight lodgers and transient hourly patrons.

The property was known as the *Sonoma House* for two years. Upon Sprigg's death in 1851, the name was changed to the *Blue Wing Inn*. One rumor motivating the change was the popularity of a San Francisco establishment with the identical name.

Among notable drinking and gambling clientele, some of California's most illustrious personalities patronized the establishment. These included Joseph Hooker, Ulysses S. Grant, William T. Sherman, John C. Fremont, bandit Joaquin Murrieta and performer Lotta Crabtree.

James C. Cooper's enterprise expanded his prosperity making him the second wealthiest man in Sonoma (after Vallejo). His good fortune and longevity however proved abruptly brief. The local schoolmaster fatally stabbed Cooper on September 5, 1856 over a dispute involving the severity of an earlier whipping administered to his two sons in class. The schoolmaster was acquitted of murder charges based on self-defense.

The Blue Wing Inn fell into gradual disrepair ceasing as a gambling hall and brothel by 1880. The building was later employed in more banal uses including a grocery and clothing store and later winemaking and storage facility.

Wine storage became its savior. A 1911 interior fire was squelched by a single wine tank causing only minor smoke damage and a scorched roof. The *Blue Wing Museum* operated on the first floor during the 1920s. The building continued to deteriorate with a succession of absentee owners and ambitious but flawed renovation projects.

The building has been designated a state landmark, but currently languishes in a perpetual state of renovation purgatory. Its presence remains nearly invisible to the incoming wine sipping, tourist and shopping throngs.

During its history, Sonoma has hoisted the national flags of Russia, Spain, Mexico, the California Republic and ultimately the United States. Amidst this volatile past, The Blue Wing Inn has persevered. The future may not remain so accommodating.

Blue Wing Inn:
131 East Spain Street, Sonoma

Caging, Rehabilitating and Labeling Prostitutes Morons and Outcast Women

In 1917, as American troops began their preparations to enter World War I, President Woodrow Wilson's *American Plan* officially forbade brothels and the sales of liquor within a five-mile radius around military bases, shipyards, munitions factories and school with military preparation programs.

In Sonoma County, public announcements declared *The State will soon build a lockup for morons who are outcast women, which is to say they are really prostitutes. P.S. Most of them will probably have chronic cases of venereal disease.*

The lockup was justified as a citizen's public duty to show support for troops and protect them against evil influences. Tens of thousands of women nationally accused of prostitution were gathered from vice raids and held in quarantine absent of due process. In Northern California, an institution called the *California Home For Feeble-Minded Children* located near Glen Ellen became their confinement quarters.

The institution was capable of imprisoning 300, but due to vocal local opposition in 1918, it was reported that *110 weak-minded girls and young women from San Francisco were quartered there.*

The dry zones ended at the conclusion of the war, but set the precedent for passage of the 21st amendment, better known as Prohibition. The battle over abolishing prostitution in California also continued to rage.

The most vocal supporters of such a plan were women's clubs that successfully lobbied to pass in April 1919 legislation that created a *California Industrial Farm for Women*. Two Sonoma locations were considered. One was J. K. Bigelow's chicken ranch (which actually raised poultry) and the 40-room mansion constructed in the 1880s on the grounds of Buena Vista winery. The state opted for the winery property and began transferring women in 1922.

At risk and *delinquent* women were sentenced to institutions for a period from six months to five years. While incarcerated, they would receive care with the stated objective of reformation. The guidelines were vague, unconstitutional and the misguided experiment farcical.

The Sonoma paper erroneously characterized the women as *dangerous* and *depraved* criminals. Suggestions were made by temperance groups to incorporate inmates from San Quentin's women's ward into the internment population fueling local outrage and paranoia. Nearly all of the women were actually in prison for non-violent crimes, primarily forgery and passing bad checks.

The concept of offering legitimate industrial or commercial training to assist reformatory aid never materialized. Instead the urban women *milked cows and painted flower boxes and pots*.

At the conclusion of 1922, fifty-four inmates remained at the facility. Seventeen were acknowledged prostitutes and the rest were considered addicts or alcoholics. All had been charged with vagrancy and one woman was reported to be 67 years old.

On March 17, 1923, the rehabilitation experiment went up in literal flames. The director and business manager were in

Sacramento, the farm manager was off duty and only a groundskeeper and attendant was present.

Cause of the fire was never officially determined, but the most prevalent theory was arson. This reason became particularly valid after an inmate proudly boasted that she had torched the structure. Feminist's groups lobbied hard for a replacement building, but despite the governor's expressed approval, the California Industrial Farm for Women ceased to exist on June 30, 1923.

For the captive, now without residence, their options became incarceration or transference to a mental asylum. Four escaped but were immediately recaptured. Five were transferred to the Napa State Mental Hospital and the balance transferred to the *California Home For Feeble-Minded Children*, renamed the *Sonoma State Home*. The Home had become a factory operation of forced sterilization and many of the women were subjected without choice to the procedure.

This entire blight of Sonoma history has been conveniently filed away and generally forgotten.

The statuesque red brick Sonoma State Home lingers vacant and decaying along with the neighboring administration mansions and patient cottages. For nearly a century, the overcrowded institution housed the mentally handicapped, the epileptic, the physically disabled, and the psychopathic delinquent. In 2015, California announced the closure of the facility aimed at the conclusion of 2018. The 2017 *Sonoma County Nuns Fire* delayed the complete transfer of patients, but the process has now been completed.

This valuable real estate in the heart of the Valley of the

Moon will eventually find a reincarnation, probably in the hospitality or wine industry. As for the Buena Vista Winery mansion, mention of this sad chapter is omitted in their historical materials. The access path to the former mansion grounds is sealed and gated preventing public access.

**California Home For Feeble-Minded Children:
15000 Arnold Drive, Eldridge**

**California Industrial Farm For Women (Buena Vista
Winery Mansion):
18000 Old Winery Road, Sonoma**

The Silent and Senseless Murder of Lindsay Cutshall and Jason Allen

Sonoma County's Russian River empties into the Pacific Ocean through a gulch severing Goat's Rock Beach and Fish Head Beach adjacent to the town of Jenner, California. Jenner, population 136, is a slumbering afterthought wedged into the winding topography of the Pacific Coast Highway (Highway 1) as motorists pass headed towards Mendocino.

If one pauses to rest in Jenner it is doubtlessly either due to the stunning panoramic views or the sheer tedium of the drive. A few modest hotel properties service the tourist clientele. August weekends are a near certainty to be fully occupied.

The route between Jenner and Mendocino features erratic patches of sunshine, even during the summer months. Tanning is not its primary appeal, rather spectacular rock formations, elevated bluffs, crashing surf and an abundant sea lion population. Such pristine and elemental beauty invites contemplation, admiration and pause for reflection.

Like generations of precedent visitors Lindsay Cutshall, 22, and her fiancé Jason S. Allen, 26, were moved by the splendor. They recorded their impressions during the sunset of August 14, 2004 in a personal travel journal.

The sun is going down in the horizon, Lindsay wrote. *All I see is the beams shining on the cliff face. And I know that God is awsome (sic). I look around and I see his creation all around me.*

Jason wrote: *As I stir this Mac & Cheese I think to myself what a wonderful life. I've just spent two awsome (sic) days with my fiancé Lindsay. Can life ever be so perfect. Only with a person who is so great. God gives me this privilege in life and He has given me a wonderful woman to enjoy it.*

Later that same evening or early the following morning, the young Midwestern couple were shot to death as they slept fully clothed in separate sleeping bags on an obscured stretch of Fish Head Beach. Their bodies were not discovered until Wednesday, August 18, when a Sheriff's helicopter was dispatched following a report of a man who was stranded on a cliff above Fish Head Beach. The helicopter spotted the bodies and notified the department.

Both Cutshall and Allen were killed with an 1894 Marlin . 45 caliber long rifle, either a long colt style, or a carbine magazine. The rifle was both uncommon and too high a caliber for common use by ranchers in the area. Shell casings were not found at the scene of the crime, suggesting the killer retrieved them.

Cutshall and Allen's travel journal with their handwritten entries were found inside a secure small wooden hutch on the beach near their makeshift campsite.

Lindsay Cutshall was from Fresno, Ohio and Jason Allen from Zeeland, Michigan. The couple met in 2002 while Cutshall was a student at Appalachian Bible College in West Virginia, and became engaged six weeks later. They planned to marry in the autumn of 2004.

During the fateful weekend of their death, they had enjoyed an impromptu getaway from the Christian youth adventure camp near Placerville where they worked. Their outing included visits to Fisherman's Wharf in San Francisco, crossing the Golden Gate Bridge and climaxed by a picturesque drive along the meandering Pacific Coast highway. They settled upon their sleeping arrangements at Fish Head Beach because on the evening of August 14, all of Jenner's accommodation properties were booked. Their selected stretch of beach was secluded and guaranteed privacy.

None of Cutshall or Allen's belongings had been taken, ruling out robbery as a motive, and neither of the campers had been sexually assaulted. Their car, a battered red *Ford Tempo* was parked in a pullout spot on the side of Highway 1 in Jenner and untouched. A silent, single bullet to the skull had executed each. The evening overcast, common to northern Sonoma County, masked the moon and neither likely had any advanced warning that they were not alone.

Camping and overnight sleeping is prohibited, but not uncommon amidst drifters and hitchhikers on the rural stretch of beach. Warning signage is evident on the primary path that leads from the highway to the beach below. Initial police speculation concentrated on a roaming drifter murdering the young couple and then leaving the area.

Crude Satanic and Dragonesque images and abundant profanity were scrawled and carved on some of the nearby bleached driftwood. When they were drawn was never determined. Over a decade later, they remain. Were the writings symbolic of a more sinister evil or merely expressions of common adolescent angst?

Despite exhaustive efforts by detectives, the scant evidence, no apparent motive, and minimal clues yielded no solid leads or publicly announced suspects for nearly fourteen years.

In May 2018, Shaun Michael Gallon, 39 was arrested and charged with the murder of the couple. He had already been in custody for two months following the killing of his younger brother Shamus in front of their mother in nearby Forestville. He was charged with attempted murder in a separate package bomb case in Monte Rio in 2004 that maimed his intended victim's wife.

While in custody, aware that he'd never know freedom again, Gallon provided the Sonoma County Sheriff's detectives with a jailhouse note indicating that he wanted to talk about the Fish Head Beach case with them. In a series of interviews, he confessed to the killings and provided information that the detectives concluded only the killer would know.

Oddly, in June 2018, Gallon pleaded *not guilty* to the murders in a preliminary Sonoma County Superior Court appearance following his confession.

His public defender created a caricature of a deeply troubled individual that had steered off course irrevocably following a 2001 excessive dose of LSD. According to an article in the *Washington Post*: On the evening of August 14, 2004 as he drove up Highway 1, Gallon was feeling upset at his own life. He decided to pull over and climb down the bluffs to the beach.

There, he saw the sleeping strangers, who he thought were homeless people. At that moment, Gallon reportedly told investigators he *snapped*, and went back to his car for the gun.

I was gonna kill them out of spite, he said.

It is nearly impossible to fell compassion towards the human wreckage that became Shaun Michael Gallon despite his possible crisis of conscience and admission of guilt. He was a familiar face to the Sonoma County Sheriff's department having been arrested on thirteen occasions. In 2013, after confronting his son with a flier about the missing murder weapon, Gallon's father reportedly committed suicide.

By pleading no contest to the first-degree murder charges at his June 2019 trial, he was spared the death penalty but sentenced to seven consecutive life terms plus additional years for various felony charges. He is currently imprisoned at San Quentin.

At 40, his remaining years may seem an eternity for a confounding series of senseless acts.

Waves habitually pound the shoreline in their custom only to recede into repetition. Tides rise and lower as they have for centuries oblivious to human existence. The stark coastal beauty reminds us that for Lindsay Cutshall and Jason Allen, their last evening together on earth served perhaps as a welcoming prelude to the paradise that their religious beliefs anticipated.

Fishhead Beach Killings:
Fishhead Beach adjacent to the town of Jenner

Downtown Petaluma: A Dual Metamorphous Upon the Banks of an Obstinate River

The Lan Mart Building:
In 1876, celebrating 100 years following America's Declaration of Independence, the Centennial Livery Stable and Cosmopolitan Hotel opened on Main Street in downtown Petaluma. Sturdy stone and brick walls formed the core of the stable that remains from a community that for many generations touted itself as the *Poultry Capital of the World*.

In the general vicinity on both sides of the street, the city hosted their own Chinatown that consisted of shacks and shanties, stores, laundries, and purportedly opium dens. The Chinese laborers had been brought to Petaluma to straighten the bends in the river, meticulously hauling away mud in wheelbarrows. Once the tortuous work was deemed completed, they were no longer welcome in the settlement.

Connecting three structures created the Lan Mart Building. The three include a livery stable, a saloon that faced Main Street and a market adjoined at the rear facing Kentucky Street. Upstairs over the livery stable were comfortable and professional chambers occupied by local prostitutes. Above, a large social hall accommodated the Moose Lodge.

At one time a passage connected the building with the three-story Cosmopolitan Hotel, constructed in 1866. The wood framed structure catered to Petaluma's working class clientele, but burned down in the 1910s. The building's footprint is currently a parking lot. The lot was employed in a memorable car scene in *American Graffiti* where a chain is affixed to a police car axle creating bedlam when the officer's commence pursuit.

The current Lan Mart compilation is the vision of a local couple that in 1969 reshaped two dilapidated buildings slated for demolition into a unique shopping mall.

McNear Building

Adjacent to the Lan Mart is the McNear Building containing a saloon, dining house and the *Mystic Theatre*. The landmark represents the legacy of the locally dynamic McNear family. In 1886, the original construction housing the *McNear's Saloon and Dining House* was completed with the adjacent building known as the *Mystic Theatre* finished in 1911. The combination has become simply known as the McNear Building. Over the years, the complex has been utilized for traditional commercial tenancies including a motorcycle shop.

The Mystic Theatre originally hosted Vaudeville entertainment and was renamed the *State Theatre* in the late 1920s. The venue was closed temporarily in the 1930s in order to install electric wiring for talking motion pictures. Over the decades, the caliber of the entertainment declined until X-rated and pornographic movies were the marquee offerings during the mid 1970s. The *State* was later reinvented as the *Plaza Theatre* showing art and foreign films until 1992 when the building was reincarnated as *The Mystic Theatre* once again. That renovation enabled live music performances with a seating capacity up to 500.

The City of Petaluma has altered its course and identity as well. No longer boasting its poultry heritage, the downtown features a hybrid of chic and boutique segwayed between the perceived sophistication of Marin and more casual rural Sonoma County ambiance. Main Street has become Petaluma Boulevard North. The Petaluma River still twists and bends despite earlier century's efforts to permanently straighten its curvatures.

Lanmart Building:
29 Petaluma Boulevard North, Petaluma

McNear's Saloon and Dining House:
23 Petaluma Boulevard North, Petaluma

Polly Klaas: The Abrupt Death of Innocence

In the autumn of 1993, Polly Klaas was a beautiful vivacious twelve-year old living with her mother and sister tranquilly in Petaluma. Her future was limitless and prospects infinite.

Richard Allen Davis had no such optimistic projections. At 39, he was a convicted felon and had spent the majority of his adult life in prison. He was living in a Bay Area halfway house as a condition of his parole. His parole officer was based in Ukiah and en route to weekly visitations, he often detoured into Petaluma. Most of his time in the city was spent loitering around Wickersham Park, located diagonally across from Polly's residence. His extended visits to the park typically involved either getting drunk or high.

It is never been determined why Davis' and Klaas' paths fatally intersected on the evening of October 1, 1993. Klaas had invited two friends over for a slumber party. Later in the evening, Davis entered her mother's house and Polly's bedroom, carrying a knife. He tied up her two friends and abducted Polly.

The circumstantial near misses in apprehending Davis over the subsequent twenty-four hours mirrored the depth of frustration the case provoked both locally and later nationally. The evening of the kidnapping, Davis was actually in conversation with two Sonoma County Sheriff officers because his car had become stuck in a ditch in a remote county sector.

Due to the limited range of their broadcasting band capabilities, the officers were unaware of the kidnapping. They assisted Davis in securing a tow truck. Despite his felony status, Davis' driver's license and plate number came back with no outstanding warrants. The deputies claimed that they did conduct a search of the car before the arrival of the tow truck due to Davis' disheveled and perspiring appearance. They specified at his trial that there was apparently no evidence of anyone additionally having been in the car.

So where was Polly Klaas?

Perhaps she had already been strangled earlier that evening and left in a temporary grave or amongst the nearby thick brush. Perhaps she sat petrified in the distance awaiting Davis' promised return. Only Davis knows and throughout his interrogations and trial, his answers were vague and inconclusive.

In all likelihood, he returned to the murder site to retrieve the body for burial in a more remote and clandestine area.

Over the next two months, a massive search for Polly Klaas was conducted and broadcast nationally. On November 28, a Sonoma County property owner was inspecting her land following a timber clearing. She found suspicious and strewn clothing and immediately contacted authorities. A massive police search effort followed and turned up additional articles.

Forensic examination linked the clothing to Klaas. With an approximate idea of her burial location, resolution of the case followed swiftly. The first investigative breakthrough in identifying the perpetrator came via a review of calls in the area the day of the kidnapping. The caller log turned up the two deputies encounter with Davis. Once his name was isolated, the case against him accelerated. A poor quality palm print had been identified at the scene of the kidnapping and matched perfectly with Davis. With his convicted felon status, he was already registered in the national crime-fingerprint database.

When you are a convicted felon, there are limited concealment options. Davis had nowhere to hide. He had nowhere to flee or disappear to. He likely wallowed in the expectation that he would ultimately be caught. His profile had already been sketched by law enforcement agencies based on the descriptions given by Polly's two friends.

Under interrogation, Davis confessed to the kidnapping. He hedged on critical details about specific timeframes, knowing his revelations could secure him a death sentence at his trial. He finally led authorities to a shallow grave just off Highway 101, about a mile south of the city limits of Cloverdale.

Despite his futile efforts at cunning and evasiveness, Richard Allen Davis was convicted on June 18, 1996 of first-degree murder and four special circumstances (robbery, burglary, kidnapping and a lewd act on a child). His lengthy trial and conviction was preceded by a change in venue due to the notoriety of the case. A San Jose Superior Court jury returned a verdict of death regardless. He had ceased to become invisible from the inevitable.

In the wake of the murder, the California legislature and several states supported three strikes legislation intended to keep violent criminals in prison for life following three felony convictions. California's Three Strikes Act was signed into law on March 8, 1994, but has since been criticized as excessive and later modified by voters.

Life strangely continues for Richard Allen Davis. He remains on death row in the East Block at San Quentin. He has already reached senior citizen status. The last California execution took place in January of 2006 and the labyrinth of appeal options will certainly delay the next.

Polly Klaas' bright future ceased abruptly on the autumn evening of October 1, 1993.

**Polly Klaas Kidnapping Site:
427 Fourth Street, Petaluma**

Ramon Salcido: The Extremities of Inhumanity

On the evening of April 14, 1989, Ramon Salcido's demons finally overwhelmed his restraint. Under the pretext of being underappreciated, he spent the evening drinking and snorting cocaine. Under the pretext of intoxication and suspecting his wife of having an affair with a coworker, he conceived the most unimaginable revenge.

He drove his three daughters, ages 22 months to four years to a county dump and slashed their throats. He left each to expire in a field. He then drove to Cotati where he killed Marion Louis Richards, his mother-in-law and two daughters. He continued his murderous spree by returning home and killing his wife Angela. He then completed the carnage by going to his workplace, the Grand Cru winery in Sonoma and killing a coworker, Tracey Toovey.

Salcido didn't allow himself an instant of reflection towards his monstrous acts. He immediately drove south and fled to Mexico via Calexico. A week later he was arrested at dawn in a surprise roadblock set up by drug enforcement agents. His capture was in a village outside of Guasave near his hometown of Los Mochis in the Sinaloa state, 850 miles northwest of Mexico City. He was transferred to the capital and extradited back to California.

His middle daughter Carmina miraculously surviving her slashing, lying in agony next to her deceased sisters for 36-hours before being discovered by a passing transient. Her survival was attributed to her keeping her head down, covering her neck wound.

At his trial, his defense sought a verdict of second-degree murder or even manslaughter citing that he was under the influence of cocaine and alcohol during the slayings. The

411

drugs his counsel contended put him in a state of psychotic depression triggering the rampage. The jury rejected this argument and convicted him on six counts of first-degree murder, one count of second-degree murder and two counts of attempted murder. He was sentenced to the death penalty and is currently incarcerated on death row at San Quentin.

One of the strangest twists to the story involved his lone surviving daughter Carmina. Adopted by an ultra conservative family in Missouri, she didn't discover the truth about her past until the age of fifteen, Her family renamed her Cecilia, but the revelation altered their relationship. At seventeen, she became a cloistered nun at Sister Mariam of Jesus Crucified in Nebraska. Less than a year later, she quit the convent and gravitated to a ranch in Idaho for troubled teenage girls.

She authored a book about her experiences and then braced herself for the ultimate confrontation, a 2006 face-to-face meeting with her father at San Quentin.

While in prison, Salcido completed a mail-in seminary class and began a prison ministry. He had begun to call himself *Reverend*. The reunion with him went poorly. He greeted her with a broad smile that she interpreted as *a joker, like a clown*. She detected no emotion or remorse from her father regarding his deeds and left the meeting unfulfilled.

On the 20/20 television program that covered the reunion, Carmina Salcido expressed revulsion for the man who destroyed her immediate family and radically altered the trajectory of her life. *I don't ever want to see him again. And I would breathe a great sigh of relief when justice has been dealt.*

Carmina ultimately returned to Sonoma County to reconstruct her life from the barest of ashes. Ramon Salcido will continue his charade as a changed man. He will never be able to reverse the damage he caused to so many.

Ramon Salcido Residence:
201 Baines Avenue, Boyes Hot Springs

The Sam Kee Laundry: Final Standing Remnant of a Friskier Napa

During the nineteenth century in California, prostitution was a tolerated institution and Napa, up until the 1930s, offered one of the largest red-light districts for any town of its size in the state.

Both sides of Clinton Street along with surrounding neighborhoods were lined with brothels. Over twenty parlors operated and none were more prestigious than May Howard's establishments. Her patrons consisted of bankers, ranch owners and other respectable professionals. Her parlors were known for their elegance, contemporary fashion and attractive women.

She had firm operational rules and standards that she rigorously maintained. She was selective in her customers and appraised each in order for them to gain admittance. Clients entered through the east side, by the railroad tracks and never through the front entrance. Men in uniform were not allowed so a change of clothing was provided outside of her business.

Her operation was considered the most profitable and respectable within Napa's *Spanish Town* and the last openly practiced service in the district when it closed in 1937.

For farm hands, laborers and cowboys, Napa's *Chinatown* red-light district became the destination for poorer patrons with inexpensive tastes.

The Sam Kee Laundry, also known as the Pfeiffer Building is located at the corner of Main and Clinton Streets in the heart of *Spanish Town*. It was constructed from hand-cut sandstone in 1875 by German immigrant Phillip Pfeiffer and is Napa's oldest stone and commercial building. The Pfeiffer began as the *Barth Brewery* until 1890 when it became the *Stone Saloon*, complete with accommodating brothel in the upper floor.

During the 1920s, it became the Sam Kee Laundry and acquired its current identity. Sam Kee contributed to Chinese-American history with his victory in a landmark court case. He successfully challenged the constitutionality of a city ordinance created in 1887 that made it illegal to have a laundry operating within city limits. The ordinance was clearly discriminatory against Chinese-Americans since they predominately managed laundry operations during the era.

From 1976 to 1999, the building housed the Andrews Meat Company and Deli. In 2002, it became the Vintner's Collective, a tasting and sales outlet for 18 local wineries without their own tasting rooms. The building features a simple stone facade design topped by a decorative Italianate cornice.

Although the August 2014 Napa earthquake damaged the facade extensively, the building was one of the fastest and most aggressively renovated. Much of the facade masonry and windows from the northeast quadrant of the building, including the entire lower level window, fell to the street below exposing the wood framing and insulation.

The Vintner's Collective operated throughout the reconstruction, re-routing their entrance through the rear. Today, the façade stones have been painstakingly refitted back into place and the structure resembles its pre-earthquake appearance.

Sam Kee Laundry and Vintner's Collective Building: 1245 Main Street, Napa

Washoe House: Gold Fever Stagecoach Stop Turned Dining Establishment

The Washoe House opened in 1859 as a stagecoach stop for pioneers and Gold Rush miners traveling to the Gold Country via Sonoma County. The roadhouse has accumulated its share of fanciful stories, colorful characters and ghostly spirits. The apparitions range from little girls to Victorian-clad figures peering at visitors from the upstairs windows.

Once its stagecoach days ended, the building housed a brothel, butcher shop and even a post office. The structure's sturdy rock foundation and redwood framing fastened by square nails survived the 1906 Earthquake intact. Few people seem aware that Sonoma County, particularly Santa Rosa suffered major destruction during the quake attributed often exclusively to San Francisco.

Fields of grazing cattle surround the border between Petaluma and Sebastopol where the Washoe is situated. The presence of encroaching grape vines loom nearby on the periphery.

The roadhouse attracts a mix of rural cowboy, bikers and urban weekenders. The cuisine matches these divergent palettes. A shared contribution each demographic has provided over the years is the bar ceiling supporting thousands of dollar bills tacked to the surface.

**Washoe House:
2840 Stony Point Road, Petaluma**

Author, photographer and visual artist Marques Vickers was born in 1957 in Vallejo, California. He graduated from Azusa Pacific University in Los Angeles and became the Public Relations and Executive Director for the Burbank, California Chamber of Commerce between 1979-84.

Professionally, he has operated travel, apparel, wine, rare book and publishing businesses. His paintings and sculptures have been exhibited in art galleries, private collections and museums in the United States and Europe. He has previously lived in the Burgundy and Languedoc regions of France and currently lives in the South Puget Sound region of Western Washington.

He has written and published over one hundred books spanning a diverse variety of subjects including true crime, international travel, social satire, wine production, architecture, history, fiction, auctions, fine art, poetry and photojournalism.

He has two daughters, Charline and Caroline who reside in Europe.

Made in the USA
Middletown, DE
03 July 2021